Everything But The Entrée

The Junior League of Parkersburg

Everything But The Entrée

A Collection of Recipes Presented by The Junior League of Parkersburg
Published by The Junior League of Parkersburg, Inc., a nonprofit organization.
The proceeds from the sale of this book will be used to support local charities.

Copyright © 1999 by
The Junior League of Parkersburg, Inc.
P.O. Box 4051
Parkersburg, West Virginia 26104

Library of Congress Number: 99-094310
ISBN: 0-9669807-0-0

Edited, designed, and manufactured by
Favorite Recipes® Press
an imprint of

FRP™

P.O. Box 305142
Nashville, Tennessee 37230
1-800-358-0560

Artwork: Robert Wren Smith
Art Director: Steve Newman
Book Design: David Malone
Project Manager: Charlene Sproles
Project Coordinator: Carolyn King

Manufactured in the United States of America
First Printing: 1999 12,500 copies

Contents

Preface

How many times are you asked to bring a side dish, dessert, or appetizer to a social function, church dinner, or committee meeting? The members of the Junior League of Parkersburg found that we were asked numerous times to do exactly that, and while we all had a few old "standbys," the tried and true recipes that would do in a pinch, we were excited to collect new ideas. You may even find a new twist to incorporate into one of your old favorites.

Our cookbook, *Everything But The Entrée,* is a collection of recipes that are easy to prepare and, of course, delicious! Today's busy cooks find those two elements in combination to be essential.

As you read the bits of history we've collected about the Junior League of Parkersburg, you will imagine many women's balancing the desire to raise strong families with being a factor of service to the community. These women embraced the community and its challenges, and decided to add their special gifts to the "recipe" for a healthy, prosperous community. You will find throughout the cookbook the "ingredients" the Junior League of Parkersburg has contributed over the years.

Thank you for your purchase of *Everything But The Entrée.* Know that you, too, are contributing to the enrichment of the lives of children in our community.

About the Artist

Robert Wren Smith has been drawing most of his life and painting in watercolor for about 20 years. He has studied with nationally known artists and attended Cincinnati Art Academy, Marietta College, and West Virginia University at Parkersburg. His work has been shown throughout the state. Smith has won many awards, including Best of Show at the West Virginia Oil & Gas Festival, 1st place award at the Regional Exhibit, Merit Award Regional 1991, Merit Award and Best of Show Aqueous Exhibit of the West Virginia Watercolor Society for 1995, Best of Show and Purchase Award at the 1998-99 Impressionist Exhibit at Townhouse Gallery. Smith is a member of Ohio Valley Artists and West Virginia Watercolor Society.

He is a retired packaging engineer from Corning, Inc. and resides with his wife, who was President of the Junior League of Parkersburg from 1991-92, and two daughters in Vienna, West Virginia.

Acknowledgements

The following women served on the Cookbook Committee, devoting many hours to making this cookbook a reality:

Suzanne Evans Beane, Chair · Tracy M. Wharton, Assistant Chair
Peg Barlament · Susan Dolinar · D'Ann Duesterhoeft McGraw
Tina Salmans · Anne Cawley Smith.

The following women contributed non-recipe text and assisted with editing:

Kim Couch · Cynthia Meyers · Mary Rossana.

Introduction

The history of the Junior League of Parkersburg, Inc., began prior to 1925 when the organization was known as the Children's Pleasure Guild. The Junior Leagues of Charleston, West Virginia, and Columbus, Ohio, sponsored the Junior League of Parkersburg as it became a member of the Association of Junior Leagues of America in 1925.

The first League maintained a slate of six officers and a Board of Managers made up of twelve women. The concerns and areas of focus of the early League consisted of volunteering at hospitals and well baby clinics, assisting the Red Cross by providing transportation for the Red Cross staff, translating manuscripts into Braille for the blind, and helping the underprivileged in various ways.

Although stated differently over the years, the mission of the League has remained the same:

1925—"The object of the League is to encourage the young women of Parkersburg to take an active interest in the efforts to solve the social problems of the city, and to maintain and increase their usefulness in their chosen service."

1999—"The Junior League of Parkersburg, Inc. is committed to promoting volunteerism and to improving the community through effective action and leadership of trained volunteers. Its purpose is educational and charitable."

The following prayer was adopted in the early years and every
League member and community volunteer should periodically stop to read and reflect on its words:

We pray that we will never be so blind
That our small world is all we see
Or so supremely satisfied, that what we are
Is all we ever hope to be.
Grant us the joy of filling someone's need
Make us gracious followers
Make gracious those who lead,
And more than all we pray
That down the years we will remember
There are always new frontiers.

Throughout the years there has always been a concern by the League for the welfare of the children of the area. From its beginning as the Children's Pleasure Guild to the present, the formal focus of the League has been "the education and enrichment of children."

The Good Cook

The Cook House was the home of Tillinghast Almy Cook and Elizabeth "Betsey" Russell Cook. Built in 1829, it is the oldest brick home in Parkersburg, West Virginia still standing in its original location.

When the Cook House was built, its Federal architectural style was very unusual for this frontier area. The two-story, inverted T-shaped house, with 8 rooms and 5 fireplaces, was quite a contrast to the prevailing rectangular one-room log homes of other settlers. The bricks, used in constructing the home, were formed from clay found on the property and were fired in a kiln also on the property.

The house remained in the possession of the Cooks and their descendants for 147 years until Elizabeth Wolfe Eddy, Tillinghast's great-granddaughter, donated the house to the Junior League of Parkersburg in 1978. Since 1986, the Junior League has maintained the house as a 19th century historical exhibit for all of our community to enjoy and treasure. In addition to hosting a Christmas Open House each December, League members also provide free tours to all fourth-grade classes in the county as a supplement to their West Virginia history studies. The Cook House is listed in the National Register of Historic Places.

Cook House 1829

Appetizers

Appetizers

Chicken Salad Puffs

1/2 cup shortening
1 cup boiling water
1/2 teaspoon salt
1 cup flour
4 eggs
1 cup finely chopped cooked
　chicken
1 cup finely chopped celery
2 tablespoons finely chopped
　pickle
2 tablespoons finely chopped
　pimento
2 tablespoons mayonnaise

Combine the shortening, water and salt in a saucepan; bring to a rolling boil. Add the flour and beat vigorously with a wooden spoon until the mixture leaves the side of the pan and forms a smooth ball. Remove from the heat. Add the eggs 1 at a time, beating well after each addition. Beat until the dough is thick and smooth. Drop the dough by teaspoonfuls 1 1/2 inches apart onto greased baking sheets.

Bake at 450 degrees for 10 minutes. Reduce the oven temperature to 350 degrees. Bake for 10 minutes or until golden brown. Cool on wire racks.

Combine the chicken, celery, pickle, pimento and mayonnaise in a bowl; mix well. Cut off the tops of the puffs and remove any soft dough in the centers. Spoon the chicken filling into the puffs and replace the tops.

Note: The puffs may be baked ahead of time and frozen.

Yield: about 4 dozen puffs

Barbecue Meatballs

1 pound ground beef
2 eggs, beaten
3/4 cup dry bread crumbs
1/4 cup minced onion
2 tablespoons minced green
   bell pepper
1/2 teaspoon salt
1/2 teaspoon Worcestershire
   sauce
1/4 teaspoon pepper
4 ounces Cheddar cheese
1/2 cup minced onion
1 cup catsup
3/4 cup water
2 tablespoons vinegar
2 tablespoons Worcestershire
   sauce
1 tablespoon sugar
1 teaspoon salt
1 teaspoon chili powder
1 teaspoon paprika
1/4 teaspoon cinnamon
1/8 teaspoon cloves

Combine the ground beef, eggs, bread crumbs, 1/4 cup onion, green pepper, 1/2 teaspoon salt, 1/2 teaspoon Worcestershire sauce and pepper in a large bowl, mixing well. Shape into thirty-six 1-inch meatballs.

Cut the cheese into 36 cubes. Press 1 cheese cube into the center of each meatball. Brown the meatballs on all sides in a large skillet over high heat; drain and set aside.

Combine 1/2 cup onion, catsup, water, vinegar, 2 tablespoons Worcestershire sauce, sugar, 1 teaspoon salt, chili powder, paprika, cinnamon and cloves in a medium saucepan, mixing well. Bring to a boil; reduce the heat to low. Simmer, uncovered, for 10 minutes.

Add the meatballs to the sauce mixture. Simmer for 10 minutes or until the meatballs are heated through. Transfer the meatballs and sauce to a chafing dish if desired and keep warm. Serve with wooden picks.

Yield: 3 dozen meatballs

Bourbon Wieners

1	3 pounds hot dogs
1/3	1 cup packed brown sugar
1/3	1 cup chili sauce
1/3	1 cup bourbon

Cut the hot dogs into bite-size pieces. Combine the hot dogs, brown sugar, chili sauce and bourbon in a large baking dish.

Bake at 325 degrees for 3 hours or until the hot dogs are slightly crispy.

Note: May also prepare this recipe in a slow cooker or make ahead and freeze for later use.

Yield: 24 servings

Marinated Mushrooms

2/3 cup vegetable oil
1/3 cup wine vinegar
1 tablespoon chopped parsley
1 tablespoon lemon juice
1 garlic clove, peeled
1/2 teaspoon sugar
1/2 teaspoon salt
1/2 teaspoon pepper
2 pounds small fresh
   mushrooms

Combine the oil, vinegar, parsley, lemon juice, garlic, sugar, salt and pepper in a glass bowl. Clean the mushrooms, leaving them whole. Add to the oil mixture, tossing to coat.

Refrigerate, covered, for 4 to 8 hours. Remove and discard the garlic. Serve the mushrooms with wooden picks.

Yield: 10 servings

Baked Ham-Stuffed Mushrooms

16 large fresh mushrooms
$1/4$ cup chopped green onions
1 tablespoon margarine or
    butter
2 teaspoons flour
$1/8$ teaspoon pepper
2 tablespoons dry white wine
2 tablespoons water
$1/2$ cup finely chopped
    cooked ham
2 tablespoons grated Parmesan
    cheese
$1/4$ cup Italian-style dry
    bread crumbs

Remove the stems from the mushrooms, reserving the caps. Chop enough of the stems to measure 1 cup.

Cook the chopped stems and green onions in the margarine in a skillet until tender. Blend in the flour and pepper. Add the wine and water. Cook until thickened and bubbly, stirring constantly. Stir in the ham and Parmesan cheese.

Fill the mushroom caps with the ham mixture. Place in a 10x15-inch baking pan. Top with the bread crumbs.

Bake at 350 degrees for 15 to 20 minutes or until the mushroom caps are tender.

Yield: 8 servings

Fold in the Community

The Junior League of Parkersburg was the first civic organization to join the Chamber of Commerce of the Greater Parkersburg Area.

Olive Balls

2 cups finely shredded
   Cheddar cheese
1 cup sifted flour
1/2 cup butter, softened
1 teaspoon paprika
4 to 5 dozen medium-size
   green olives stuffed with
   pimento (Spanish-style
   olives)

Combine the cheese, flour, butter and paprika in a bowl and blend well. Roll into walnut-size balls, enclosing an olive in each ball. Place on baking sheets.

Bake at 400 degrees for 15 minutes.

Yield: 4 to 5 dozen olive balls

Try

Rumaki

1/4 cup soy sauce
1/4 cup bourbon
12 chicken livers, cut into
   halves
12 water chestnuts, cut into
   halves
Brown sugar
12 slices bacon, cut into halves

Combine the soy sauce and bourbon in a bowl. Add the chicken livers, stirring to coat. Refrigerate, covered, for 4 hours.

Remove the chicken livers from the marinade and drain on paper towels. Discard the marinade. Cut a slit in each liver half.

Insert a water chestnut half into the slit in each liver. Roll the stuffed livers in brown sugar, pressing the sugar onto the livers to coat.

Place each liver on 1 end of a bacon piece and roll up. Secure with a wooden pick. Place on a jelly roll pan. Sprinkle with additional brown sugar.

Bake at 400 degrees for 20 to 30 minutes or until the bacon and livers are cooked through, turning occasionally.

Note: May be assembled a day in advance, tightly covered and refrigerated. Bake just before serving.

Yield: 24 rumaki

4th July 2000 Made impossible pie w sausage — good

Sausage-Cheese Balls

1 pound bulk pork sausage
  (mild or hot)
1 pound sharp Cheddar cheese,
  shredded
3 cups baking mix

Combine $^1/_2$ pound of the sausage, $^1/_2$ pound of the cheese and $1^1/_2$ cups of the baking mix in a bowl. Shape into balls the size of large marbles. Place in a large baking pan. Repeat with the remaining $^1/_2$ pound sausage, $^1/_2$ pound cheese and $1^1/_2$ cups baking mix.

Bake at 350 degrees for 15 minutes or until golden brown and cooked through.

Note: May be frozen after baking. To serve, wrap in foil and reheat.

Yield: 100 sausage balls

Pinwheel Appetizers

2 (10-ounce) packages frozen
  chopped spinach, thawed,
  well drained
8 ounces cream cheese,
  softened
1 cup light sour cream
1 (3-ounce) jar real bacon bits
  or 1 (4-ounce) can diced
  green chiles, drained
$^1/_2$ (2-ounce) envelope ranch
  party dip mix
3 green onions, chopped
8 to 10 flour tortillas
  (8 to 10 inches)

Squeeze the spinach between paper towels to remove any excess liquid. Combine the spinach, cream cheese, sour cream, bacon bits, dip mix and green onions in a bowl; mix well.

Spread the spinach mixture over the tortillas to within $^3/_4$ inch of the edge. Roll up the tortillas carefully and wrap in plastic wrap. Refrigerate for 8 to 10 hours.

Cut the tortilla rolls crosswise into $^1/_2$-inch slices to serve.

Yield: 16 to 20 servings

Sensational Spinach Balls

2 (10-ounce) packages frozen
 chopped spinach, thawed,
 well drained
2 cups bread crumbs
1 large onion, finely chopped
3/4 cup grated Romano cheese
4 eggs, beaten
3/4 cup melted margarine or
 butter
Salt and pepper to taste

Combine the spinach and bread crumbs in a bowl; mix well. Add the onion, Romano cheese, eggs, margarine, salt and pepper and blend well. Refrigerate, covered, until chilled.

Shape the spinach mixture into balls. Place on a baking sheet.

Bake at 375 degrees for 20 minutes. Drain on paper towels. Roll in additional Romano cheese while hot.

Yield: about 70 spinach balls

Zucchini Fritters

1 1/2 cups shredded unpeeled
 zucchini
1/4 cup grated Parmesan cheese
1/4 cup flour
2 eggs
2 tablespoons finely chopped
 onion
2 tablespoons mayonnaise
1/4 teaspoon oregano
Salt and pepper to taste
1/4 cup vegetable oil

Combine the zucchini, Parmesan cheese, flour, eggs, onion, mayonnaise, oregano, salt and pepper in a bowl; mix well.

Heat the vegetable oil in a large skillet until hot. Drop the zucchini mixture by tablespoonfuls into the hot oil. Cook until browned on both sides. Serve immediately.

Yield: about 30 fritters

Green Chile Pie

2 (4-ounce) cans whole green
  chiles, drained
12 ounces shredded Monterey
  Jack cheese
4 eggs, beaten

Split the chiles lengthwise into halves. Line a 9-inch pie plate with the chile halves. Sprinkle with the cheese. Pour the eggs over the cheese and chiles.

Bake at 350 degrees for 40 minutes or until a knife inserted in the center comes out clean.

Note: May be frozen before baking. To thaw, heat on the lower oven rack at 350 degrees for 15 minutes. Bake as directed.

Yield: 16 servings

Spinach Squares

1 (10-ounce) package frozen
  chopped spinach, thawed,
  well drained
1 cup flour
1 cup milk
1 cup shredded Cheddar cheese
2 eggs, beaten
1/2 cup melted butter
1/2 cup chopped onion
  (optional)
1 teaspoon baking powder
1 teaspoon salt

Combine the spinach, flour, milk, cheese, eggs, butter, onion, baking powder and salt in a bowl, mixing well. Spoon into a greased 9x13-inch baking pan, spreading evenly.

Bake at 350 degrees for 30 minutes or until a knife inserted in the center comes out clean. Cool slightly before cutting into small squares. Serve alone or on top of crackers.

Yield: 20 servings

Hot-Sweet-Spicy Roasted Pecans

1¹/₂ teaspoons ground
   pasilla chile
1 teaspoon sugar
³/₄ teaspoon salt
¹/₂ teaspoon ground coriander
¹/₂ teaspoon cumin seeds
¹/₂ teaspoon ginger
¹/₂ teaspoon cayenne pepper
¹/₄ teaspoon ground cloves
1 egg white
3 cups pecan halves

Combine the pasilla chile, sugar, salt, coriander, cumin seeds, ginger, cayenne and cloves in a large bowl. Add the egg white and pecans and stir to coat well. Spread the pecan mixture on a buttered baking sheet.

Bake at 400 degrees for about 20 minutes or until the pecans are toasted.

Note: May substitute ³/₄ teaspoon paprika and ¹/₄ teaspoon cayenne pepper for the pasilla chile and omit the ¹/₂ teaspoon cayenne pepper.

Yield: 3 cups

Gently Combine Generations

Projects that enhanced the lives of the older population in Parkersburg included a year-long "Senior Special Events" project that held 12 monthly events providing educational, cultural, and social interaction for over 700 senior citizens.

Another project of interest was a lecture series held in conjunction with the local community college that addressed the concerns and dynamics of aging. And in League year 1081-82, League volunteers staffed a medical room at the local Senior Citizens Center.

Autumn Apple Dip

6 ounces cream cheese,
  softened
1/2 cup packed brown sugar
1/4 cup sugar
1 teaspoon vanilla extract

Combine the cream cheese, brown sugar, sugar and vanilla in a bowl, mixing well. Serve with sliced Granny Smith apples.

Yield: 12 servings

Fresh Fruit Dip

2 tablespoons butter
2 tablespoons flour
2/3 cup pineapple juice
2 eggs, beaten
2/3 cup sugar
2 cups whipped topping

Melt the butter in a small saucepan. Add the flour, stirring until smooth. Stir in the pineapple juice gradually. Cook over low heat until thickened and bubbly, stirring constantly. Remove from the heat; cool slightly.

Stir in the eggs and sugar. Cook over low heat until hot and thickened. Remove from the heat. Cool at room temperature for 1 hour.

Fold in the whipped topping. Refrigerate, covered, for 1 hour before serving. Serve with assorted fruit, such as strawberries, apples, pears, bananas and grapes.

Yield: 30 servings

Pineapple Cheese Dip

16 ounces cream cheese,
  softened
1 (8-ounce) can crushed
  pineapple, drained
1/4 cup chopped green bell
  pepper
2 tablespoons chopped onion
1 teaspoon seasoned salt
1 fresh pineapple

Combine the cream cheese, crushed pineapple, green pepper, onion and seasoned salt in a medium bowl, mixing well.

Slice the fresh pineapple lengthwise into halves. Remove and discard the core. Cut the pineapple flesh into chunks and scoop out leaving empty pineapple shells. Reserve the pineapple for another use.

Spoon the cheese mixture into 1 of the pineapple shells. Serve with your favorite crackers.

Yield: 30 servings

Artichoke Parmesan Dip

Try

1 cup mayonnaise
1 cup grated Parmesan cheese
1 cup artichoke hearts, chopped
1 garlic clove, minced (optional)

Combine the mayonnaise, Parmesan cheese, artichoke hearts and garlic in a bowl; mix well. Spoon into a small baking dish.

Bake at 350 degrees for 30 minutes or until browned and heated through.

Note: For a lower fat version, substitute 1 cup reduced-fat mayonnaise and 1/2 cup egg substitute for the regular mayonnaise. For a carrot version, substitute 1 cup finely shredded carrots for the artichoke hearts.

Yield: 24 servings

Tex-Mex Relish

1 (15-ounce) can black beans,
  drained
1 (7-ounce) can niblet corn
$^{1}/_{4}$ cup balsamic vinegar
$^{1}/_{4}$ cup chopped sweet onion
1 (4-ounce) can chopped
  green chiles
1 tablespoon Dijon mustard

Combine the black beans, undrained corn, vinegar, onion, undrained chiles and mustard in a bowl. Refrigerate, covered, for at least 2 hours. Serve with tortilla chips.

Yield: 24 servings

Black Bean Dip

1 (15-ounce) can black beans,
  rinsed, drained
$^{1}/_{2}$ cup chopped onion
2 garlic cloves, minced
1 teaspoon vegetable oil
$^{1}/_{2}$ cup diced tomatoes
$^{1}/_{3}$ cup mild picante sauce
$^{1}/_{2}$ teaspoon cumin
$^{1}/_{2}$ teaspoon chili powder
$^{1}/_{4}$ cup shredded reduced-fat
  Monterey Jack cheese
$^{1}/_{4}$ cup chopped fresh cilantro
1 tablespoon fresh lime juice

Mash the black beans in a bowl until chunky; set aside.

Sauté the onion and garlic in the oil in a nonstick skillet over medium heat for 4 minutes or until tender. Add the mashed beans, tomatoes, picante sauce, cumin and chili powder. Cook for 5 minutes or until thick, stirring constantly.

Remove from the heat. Add the cheese, cilantro and lime juice and mix well. Serve warm or at room temperature with tortilla chips.

Yield: 24 servings

The Building Blocks of a Good Recipe

Throughout the history of the Junior League of Parkersburg, there has always been interest and support of endeavors for new and improved facilities for children and the community. These endeavors include renovations to the City Park Pavilion, the Carnegie Library/Wood County Library, the Girl Scout lodge at Camp Sandy Bend, the Building Fund for the Wood County Society for Crippled Children's Treatment Center, a project to review the Department of Public Health's building, children's swings for the park, building of an area playground, the Mid-Ohio Valley Fellowship Home, and many more. The League has given volunteer time and/or financial assistance to all of these projects.

In addition to these projects, the League annually maintains their headquarters —the Cook House —a historical landmark used in the 4th grade history curriculum of Wood County through tours and activity books. League members are solely responsible for the upkeep and maintenance of this home and also give all the tours and create all of the activity books.

Cowboy Caviar

1 (15-ounce) can black beans,
  rinsed, drained
1 (4-ounce) can black olives,
  rinsed, drained
1 small onion, finely chopped
1 garlic clove, minced
2 tablespoons vegetable oil
2 tablespoons lime juice
$1/4$ teaspoon salt
$1/4$ teaspoon crushed red pepper
$1/4$ teaspoon cumin
$1/8$ teaspoon black pepper
8 ounces cream cheese,
  softened
2 hard-cooked eggs, chopped

Combine the black beans, olives, onion, garlic, oil, lime juice, salt, red pepper, cumin and black pepper in a bowl. Refrigerate, covered, for up to 2 days before serving.

Spread the cream cheese on the bottom of a 9-inch pie plate. Top with the bean mixture. Arrange the eggs on top and around the edge. Garnish with green onions. Serve with tortilla chips.

Yield: 30 servings

A Bushel of Members

The average attendance was 101 at each of the nine membership meetings held in League year 1982-1983.

Just Caliente Taco Dip

1 pound ground beef
1 envelope taco seasoning mix
1 (16-ounce) can refried beans
1 (4-ounce) can chopped
    green chiles
1 pound shredded Cheddar
    cheese
1 (12-ounce) bottle taco sauce

Brown the ground beef in a skillet, stirring until crumbly; drain. Stir in the taco seasoning mix. Cook according to the seasoning mix package directions; set aside.

Spread the beans in a 9x13-inch pan. Top with the beef mixture. Layer the undrained chiles, cheese and taco sauce over the beef.

Bake at 375 degrees for 30 minutes or until heated through. Serve with tortilla chips.

Yield: 24 servings

Homemade Summer Tomato Salsa

$5^1/2$ pounds medium tomatoes,
    peeled, diced
2 onions, diced
1 (7-ounce) can diced
    green chiles
$1/2$ cup vinegar
2 tablespoons lemon juice
2 tablespoons chopped
    fresh cilantro
2 teaspoons salt
$1^1/2$ teaspoons cayenne pepper
1 teaspoon black pepper

Combine the tomatoes, onions, undrained chiles, vinegar, lemon juice, cilantro, salt, cayenne and black pepper in a saucepan. Cook until heated through. Cool slightly. Refrigerate, covered, until chilled.

Note: For best results, use vine-ripened summer tomatoes.

Yield: 4 quarts

Black-Eyed Pea and Corn Salsa

2 tablespoons olive oil
2 tablespoons red wine vinegar
2 tablespoons honey
3/4 teaspoon salt
1/2 teaspoon pepper
1 cup diced celery
1 cup diced red bell pepper
1/3 cup diced onion
3 tablespoons chopped
   fresh cilantro
1 tablespoon minced jalapeño
   pepper, seeds removed
2 (15-ounce) cans black-eyed
   peas, rinsed, drained
2 (15-ounce) cans niblet corn,
   drained

Combine the oil, vinegar, honey, salt and pepper in a small bowl. Whisk until the honey is thoroughly blended; set aside.

Combine the celery, red pepper, onion, cilantro and jalapeño pepper in a bowl. Add the black-eyed peas and corn. Mix gently to combine.

Pour the honey mixture over the vegetable mixture. Stir with a rubber spatula. Refrigerate, covered, until chilled.

Note: May be prepared a day in advance.

Yield: 7 to 8 cups

Creamy Corn Dip

1 (15-ounce) can Shoe Peg
    corn
1 cup mayonnaise
1 cup sour cream
1 cup finely shredded
    Cheddar cheese
1 small onion, finely chopped
1 (4-ounce) can chopped green
    chiles, drained (optional)
$^1/_8$ to $^1/_4$ teaspoon cayenne
    pepper

Combine the undrained corn, mayonnaise, sour cream, cheese, onion, chiles and cayenne pepper in a bowl. Refrigerate, covered, for 1 hour or until chilled. Serve with corn chips.

Yield: 36 servings

Hot Virginia Dip

1 cup chopped pecans
2 teaspoons butter
16 ounces cream cheese,
    softened
1 cup sour cream
5 ounces dried beef, minced
$^1/_4$ cup milk
4 teaspoons minced onion
1 teaspoon garlic salt

Sauté the pecans in the butter in a skillet until golden brown; set aside.

Combine the cream cheese, sour cream, dried beef, milk, onion and garlic salt in a bowl; mix well. Spoon into a $1^1/_2$-quart baking dish. Sprinkle with the pecans.

Bake at 350 degrees for 20 minutes. Serve hot with crackers or breadsticks.

Note: May be assembled in advance, covered and refrigerated. Bake just before serving.

Yield: 30 servings

Bread Bowl Beef Dip

16 ounces cream cheese,
  softened
1 cup sour cream
1/2 cup chopped green
  bell pepper
2 tablespoons milk
2 tablespoons instant minced
  onion
1/2 teaspoon salt
3 ounces dried beef
1 round loaf bread
1/4 cup chopped toasted pecans
  (optional)

Blend the cream cheese and sour cream in a bowl. Add the green pepper, milk, onion and salt and mix well. Tear the dried beef into small pieces. Stir into the cheese mixture. Spoon into a 1-quart baking dish.

Bake at 350 degrees for 25 minutes or until heated through.

Hollow out the center of the bread loaf. Spoon the hot dip into the center of the bread. Sprinkle with the pecans. Tear the bread removed from the center into pieces and serve with the dip.

Yield: 30 servings

A Dash of Politics

Mrs. Sharon Rockefeller, wife of former Governor John D. Rockefeller IV, joined the League at the April 1980 meeting and spoke on the topic "The Role of a Governor's Wife."

Try

Crab-Cheese Dip

2 tablespoons chopped onion
2 tablespoons chopped green
  bell pepper
2 tablespoons margarine or
  butter
1 (10-ounce) can cream of
  mushroom soup
$1/2$ cup milk
6 ounces shredded Cheddar
  cheese
2 eggs
1 (7-ounce) can crab meat,
  drained
$1/8$ teaspoon nutmeg

Sauté the onion and green pepper in the margarine in a skillet until tender but not brown. Stir in the soup gradually. Blend in the milk. Cook until bubbly, stirring constantly. Add the cheese, stirring until melted.

Beat the eggs in a bowl. Add a moderate amount of the hot cheese mixture gradually, stirring constantly. Stir the egg mixture gradually into the remaining cheese mixture. Cook until bubbly, stirring constantly.

Add the crab meat and nutmeg and mix well. Serve warm with crackers.

Yield: 24 servings

Gouda Cheese Appetizer

1 (8-ounce) round Gouda
  cheese
1 (5-count) can buttermilk
  biscuits
Honey mustard

Remove and discard the wax covering from the cheese. Press the biscuits together to form a circle large enough to completely encase the cheese.

Spread the mustard over the surface of the biscuit circle. Place the cheese in the center. Bring the edge of the biscuit dough up and over the cheese to cover completely, pinching the dough at the top to seal. Place in a decorative pie plate or baking dish.

Bake at 350 degrees for 20 minutes. Serve with crackers.

Yield: 8 to 10 servings

Cream Cheese Chicken Ball

8 ounces cream cheese,
  softened
1 (6-ounce) can chunk white
  chicken
$1/4$ cup chicken broth
1 tablespoon minced onion
1 tablespoon minced celery
1 tablespoon chopped green
  bell pepper
Onion powder to taste
Celery salt to taste

Combine the cream cheese, undrained chicken, broth, onion, celery, green pepper, onion powder and celery salt in a bowl; mix well. Shape into a ball.

Refrigerate, covered, until firm. Serve with crackers.

Yield: 12 servings

Vegetable Cheesecake

1 (5-ounce) package thin
    vegetable crackers
$1/3$ cup melted butter or
    margarine
16 ounces cream cheese,
    softened
$1/2$ cup finely chopped
    broccoli florets
$1/2$ cup finely chopped red
    bell pepper
$1/3$ cup grated Parmesan cheese
$1/4$ cup finely chopped
    green onions
2 teaspoons ranch salad
    dressing mix
$1/4$ teaspoon garlic powder
$1/8$ teaspoon Worcestershire
    sauce

Process the crackers in a food processor container until fine crumbs form (about $1^1/2$ cups crumbs). Combine the cracker crumbs and butter in a bowl; mix well. Press onto the bottom of a 9-inch springform pan.

Beat the cream cheese in a mixer bowl at medium speed until smooth. Add the broccoli, red pepper, Parmesan cheese, green onions, salad dressing mix, garlic powder and Worcestershire sauce and mix well. Spread over the cracker crust.

Refrigerate, covered, for 8 hours. Remove the side from the pan. Place the cheesecake on a serving platter. Serve with party rye bread or crackers.

Yield: 12 servings

Quick Braunschweiger Pâté

1 pound braunschweiger
1/2 cup unsalted butter,
  softened
4 ounces cream cheese,
  softened
6 slices bacon, crisp-cooked,
  crumbled
5 green onions, minced
Worcestershire sauce to taste
Freshly ground pepper to taste

Bring the braunschweiger to room temperature. Combine the braunschweiger, butter, cream cheese, bacon and green onions in a bowl until well blended. Stir in the Worcestershire sauce and pepper. Spoon into a serving bowl.

Refrigerate, covered, until chilled. Serve with crackers or toasts.

Note: May spoon pâté into a bowl lined with plastic wrap. Chill and unmold onto a serving plate.

Yield: 6 to 8 servings

A Measure of Compassion

In the early eighties when the hospice movement began sweeping the country, the Junior League of Parkersburg took up the cause locally.

What started as a four-phase project to research, study, and evaluate the need for a program of specialized care for terminally ill patients and their families later resulted in the Hospice Association of the Greater Parkersburg Area. In 1984, the League recruited nine people to serve on the original Board of Directors.

Today, Hospice of Parkersburg continues to provide comfort and assistance to the terminally ill and their families.

Salmon Pecan Balls

1 (16-ounce) can red salmon,
    drained, flaked
8 ounces cream cheese,
    softened
1 tablespoon lemon juice
2 teaspoons grated onion
1 teaspoon horseradish
1/4 teaspoon salt
1/4 teaspoon liquid smoke
1/2 cup chopped pecans
3 tablespoons snipped
    fresh parsley

Remove and discard any skin and bones from the salmon. Combine the salmon, cream cheese, lemon juice, onion, horseradish, salt and liquid smoke in a bowl, mixing well. Refrigerate, covered, for 3 to 4 hours.

Combine the pecans and parsley in a bowl. Shape the salmon mixture into balls. Roll the balls in the pecan mixture to coat. Refrigerate, covered, until chilled.

Yield: 20 servings

Seafood Mousse

1 envelope unflavored gelatin
$^1/_2$ cup cold water
$^3/_4$ cup hot water
1 tablespoon vinegar
1 teaspoon salt
$^1/_2$ teaspoon paprika
$^3/_4$ cup drained canned tuna, flaked
$^1/_4$ cup finely chopped celery
$^1/_4$ cup finely chopped cucumber

Soften the gelatin in the cold water in a bowl. Add the hot water; stir until dissolved. Stir in the vinegar, salt and paprika. Cool until the gelatin begins to set. Stir in the tuna, celery and cucumber.

Spoon into a greased 3-cup mold. Refrigerate, covered, for 2 hours or until firm. Unmold onto a lettuce-lined serving plate. Serve with crackers.

Note: May substitute salmon for the tuna.

Yield: 24 servings

Breads

Breads

Try

Yummy Yeast Biscuits

1 envelope dry yeast
2 tablespoons warm water
   (105 to 115 degrees)
5 cups flour
$1/4$ cup sugar
1 tablespoon baking powder
1 teaspoon baking soda
1 teaspoon salt
1 cup shortening
2 cups buttermilk

Dissolve the yeast in the warm water in a cup; set aside.

Combine the flour, sugar, baking powder, baking soda and salt in a bowl. Cut in the shortening until the mixture resembles coarse crumbs.

Combine the yeast mixture and buttermilk in a separate bowl. Add to the flour mixture and mix well to form a dough. Knead 4 to 5 times on a lightly floured surface.

Roll out the dough to a $1/2$-inch thickness. Cut with a biscuit cutter. Place the biscuits on a greased baking sheet.

Bake at 400 degrees for 12 to 15 minutes or until golden brown.

Yield: 12 to 15 biscuits

Try

Cinnamon Teatime Scones

2 cups flour
$^1/_4$ cup sugar
2 teaspoons baking powder
$1^1/_2$ teaspoons cinnamon
$^1/_2$ teaspoon salt
$^1/_8$ teaspoon cloves
$^1/_4$ cup shortening
$^1/_2$ cup buttermilk *or crème?*

crème

Combine the flour, sugar, baking powder, cinnamon, salt and cloves in a bowl; mix well. Cut in the shortening with a pastry blender until the mixture resembles coarse crumbs. Stir in the buttermilk.

Shape the dough into a ball. Cut into 12 equal pieces and shape each piece into a ball. Place 2 inches apart on a greased and floured baking sheet. Flatten each ball to a $^3/_4$-inch thickness. Brush the tops with additional buttermilk and sprinkle with sugar if desired.

Bake at 425 degrees for 10 minutes or until lightly browned.

Yield: 12 scones

Golden Corn Bread

1 cup yellow cornmeal
1 cup flour
1/4 cup sugar
4 teaspoons baking powder
1/2 teaspoon salt
1 cup skim milk
1/4 cup vegetable oil
1 egg

Combine the cornmeal, flour, sugar, baking powder and salt in a large bowl. Beat the milk, oil and egg in a separate bowl for 1 minute. Add to the dry ingredients; stir just until mixed. Pour into a greased 9-inch cast-iron skillet.

Bake at 425 degrees for 20 to 25 minutes or until a wooden pick inserted in the center comes out clean. Serve warm with butter or covered with creamed chicken.

Note: May also bake in greased muffin pans. Reduce the baking time accordingly.

Yield: 6 servings

A Peck of Education

In 1951, the Junior League of Parkersburg joined other West Virginia Junior Leagues to establish a Social Welfare Scholarship Fund to benefit a deserving graduate student at West Virginia University. This scholarship fund continued for several years.

Governor Ann Richards' Jalapeño Cheese Corn Bread

1 1/2 cups corn bread mix
3/4 cup shredded sharp Cheddar
   cheese
3/4 cup milk
1/2 cup cream-style corn
1/4 cup chopped jalapeño
   peppers
1 egg
2 tablespoons vegetable oil
1 tablespoon sugar
1/2 green onion, chopped
Bacon bits to taste
Minced garlic to taste
Pimento to taste

Combine the corn bread mix, cheese, milk, corn, jalapeño peppers, egg, oil, sugar, green onion, bacon, garlic and pimento in a bowl, mixing well. Pour into a greased 9-inch square baking pan.

Bake at 425 degrees for 25 minutes or until a wooden pick inserted in the center comes out clean.

Yield: 9 servings

Try

Banana Nut Bread

2 cups flour
1 1/3 cups sugar
1 teaspoon baking powder
1 teaspoon baking soda
3/4 teaspoon salt
1 cup mashed ripe bananas
1/2 cup shortening
1/2 cup milk
1/2 cup buttermilk
2 eggs
1/2 cup chopped pecans or
   walnuts

Sift the flour, sugar, baking powder, baking soda and salt into a mixer bowl. Add the bananas, shortening, milk and buttermilk. Beat for 2 minutes on low to medium speed. Add the eggs. Beat for 1 minute. Stir in the pecans. Pour into a greased and floured 5x9-inch loaf pan.

Bake at 350 degrees for 45 to 50 minutes or until a wooden pick inserted in the center comes out clean. Cool in the pan for 10 minutes. Remove from the pan and cool completely on a wire rack.

Yield: 12 servings

A Measure of Milk

The milk fund began in 1926 to assist thousands of needy families. During the course of this project, several hundred thousand pints of milk were distributed. Families participating in this program were seen monthly in the Well Baby Clinic.

Cranberry Orange Bread

3/4 cup orange juice
1/3 cup vegetable oil
2 eggs
2 cups flour
1 cup rolled oats
3/4 cup sugar
2 teaspoons baking powder
1/2 teaspoon baking soda
1/2 teaspoon salt
1 tablespoon grated orange zest
3/4 cup chopped cranberries
1/2 cup chopped pecans or
  walnuts

Beat the orange juice, oil and eggs in a large bowl. Combine the flour, oats, sugar, baking powder, baking soda, salt and orange zest in a medium bowl; mix well. Add to the orange juice mixture; stir just until mixed. Fold in the cranberries and pecans. Pour into a greased and floured 5x9-inch loaf pan.

Bake at 350 degrees for 1 hour or until a wooden pick inserted in the center comes out clean. Cool in the pan for 10 minutes. Remove from the pan and cool completely on a wire rack.

Yield: 12 servings

A Skosh of Vision

Literacy and the importance of reading has been an area of Junior League interest from 1925-1998. From the first year of its existence, the League was transcribing manuscripts into Braille. In the early eighties the League sponsored a project to increase the number of books in the Wood County Public Library to stimulate readership and develop a new library program.

This was a very successful project that resulted in 300 new books available to the public. And even today the League is reviewing the feasibility of a new project to promote literacy from birth, starting in the hospital with new mothers.

Pumpkin Spice Bread

3¹/2 cups flour
2¹/2 cups sugar
2 teaspoons baking soda
1¹/2 teaspoons salt
1 teaspoon cinnamon
1 teaspoon nutmeg
1 (16-ounce) can pumpkin
1 cup corn oil
4 eggs

Combine the flour, sugar, baking soda, salt, cinnamon and nutmeg in a large bowl; mix well. Blend the pumpkin and oil in a separate bowl. Add the eggs 1 at a time, beating well after each addition. Make a well in the center of the flour mixture. Pour the pumpkin mixture into the well. Stir just until the dry ingredients are moistened. Pour into 2 greased and floured 5x9-inch loaf pans.

Bake at 350 degrees for 1 hour or until a wooden pick inserted in the center comes out clean. Cool in the pans for 10 minutes. Remove from the pans and cool completely on wire racks.

Yield: 24 servings

Polish Baker's Nut Rolls

1/4 cup warm water (105 to
  115 degrees)
2 envelopes dry yeast
1 teaspoon sugar
6 cups flour
1/2 cup sugar
1 teaspoon salt
1 cup butter
5 egg yolks, beaten
1 (12-ounce) can evaporated
  milk
1 pound walnuts, ground
1 cup sugar
3/4 cup evaporated milk
1/4 cup butter, softened
1 teaspoon vanilla extract
1 egg, beaten
3 (12-ounce) jars poppy seed
  filling

Combine the water, yeast and 1 teaspoon sugar in a small bowl; stir to dissolve the yeast. Let stand at room temperature for 10 to 15 minutes or until doubled.

Sift the flour, 1/2 cup sugar and salt into a large bowl. Cut in 1 cup butter with a pastry blender until the mixture resembles coarse crumbs.

Combine the egg yolks and 12 ounces evaporated milk in a bowl. Stir into the yeast mixture. Add the milk mixture to the flour mixture; stir to form a dough.

Turn the dough out onto a lightly floured surface. Knead for 10 minutes or until smooth and elastic. Place the dough in a large bowl and cover with foil. Refrigerate for 4 to 24 hours or until doubled.

Combine the walnuts, 1 cup sugar, 3/4 cup evaporated milk, 1/4 cup butter and vanilla in a bowl, mixing well.

Divide the dough into 4 equal pieces. Roll each piece on a floured surface to a 7x12-inch rectangle. Brush the surface of each rectangle with the beaten egg. Top 2 of the rectangles with the nut mixture and the remaining 2 with the poppy seed filling, spreading to within 1/2 inch of the edges. Roll up the rectangles jelly roll style, starting from a long side, to form 12-inch rolls. Place the rolls on lightly greased baking sheets. Cover with towels and let rise in a warm place for 30 minutes or until doubled.

Bake at 325 degrees for 30 to 45 minutes or until golden brown. Cool on wire racks. Cut into 1-inch slices to serve.

Note: May add 1 cup raisins to the poppy seed filling.

Yield: 48 servings

Spinach Orange Bread with Strawberry Cheese

2 cups fresh spinach leaves, stems removed
$1/2$ medium orange
3 extra-large eggs
$1^3/4$ cups sugar
1 cup vegetable oil
3 cups flour
1 teaspoon baking soda
1 teaspoon salt
$1/2$ teaspoon baking powder
$1/4$ teaspoon cinnamon
$1/4$ teaspoon nutmeg
16 ounces cream cheese, softened
2 tablespoons milk
$1/2$ cup strawberry preserves

Wash the spinach; drain well. Cut into $1/4$-inch pieces.

Cut the orange into chunks. Grind both the pulp and peel in a blender container.

Beat the eggs in a mixer bowl. Add the sugar and oil and mix well. Blend in the spinach and orange.

Sift the flour, baking soda, salt, baking powder, cinnamon and nutmeg together. Add to the spinach mixture and stir gently. Pour into 2 greased 5x9-inch loaf pans.

Bake at 350 degrees for 45 to 50 minutes or until a wooden pick inserted in the center comes out clean. Cool in the pans for 10 minutes. Remove from the pans and cool completely on wire racks.

Beat the cream cheese in a mixer bowl until smooth and creamy. Blend in the milk. Add the preserves and mix well.

Slice the bread thinly. Cut into shapes if desired. Spread with the strawberry cream cheese. Top with additional bread slices to form sandwiches if desired.

Note: Delicious served with Roasted Pecan Chicken Salad (page 98).

Yield: 48 servings

Zucchini Walnut Bread

1 cup vegetable oil
3 eggs, beaten
2 cups sugar
3 cups flour
1 tablespoon cinnamon
1 teaspoon baking soda
1 teaspoon salt
1/4 teaspoon baking powder
2 cups shredded zucchini
1 cup chopped walnuts
2 teaspoons vanilla extract

Combine the oil, eggs and sugar in a bowl, mixing well. Stir in the flour, cinnamon, baking soda, salt and baking powder. Fold in the zucchini, walnuts and vanilla. Pour into 2 greased 5x9-inch loaf pans.

Bake at 350 degrees for 1 hour and 10 minutes. Cool in the pans for 10 minutes. Remove from the pans and cool completely on wire racks.

Yield: 24 servings

Fabulous Focaccia

1 cup warm water
   (110 degrees)
1 envelope dry yeast
1 tablespoon sugar
$1/3$ cup olive oil
$1/4$ cup sugar
1 teaspoon salt
3 to $3^1/2$ cups flour
$1/2$ cup sautéed chopped onion,
   cooled
$1/4$ cup chopped sun-dried
   tomatoes
$1/4$ cup olive oil
$1/4$ cup wine vinegar
2 teaspoons sugar
$1^1/2$ teaspoons balsamic vinegar
1 teaspoon crushed garlic
1 teaspoon basil
6 ounces grated asiago cheese
Rosemary to taste

Combine the water, yeast and 1 tablespoon sugar in a large bowl; stir to dissolve the yeast. Let stand at room temperature until foamy. Stir in $1/3$ cup olive oil and $1/4$ cup sugar. Add the salt. Stir in the flour gradually until a dough forms that pulls away from the side of the bowl. Stir in the onion and sun-dried tomatoes.

Turn the dough onto a lightly floured surface. Knead gently for 7 to 10 minutes or until smooth and elastic. Place the dough in an oiled bowl. Cover and let rise in a warm place until doubled.

Punch down the dough. Roll out on a floured surface to $1/4$- to $1/2$-inch thickness. Place on a greased baking sheet. Make depressions in the surface of the dough with the handle of a wooden spoon or fingertips. Combine $1/4$ cup olive oil, wine vinegar, 2 teaspoons sugar, balsamic vinegar, garlic and basil in a bowl; mix well. Brush half the oil mixture over the surface of the dough.

Bake at 375 degrees for 5 minutes. Brush with the remaining oil mixture. Bake for 5 minutes longer. Sprinkle with the cheese and rosemary. Bake for 3 to 5 minutes or until golden brown. Watch carefully to prevent the cheese from burning.

Yield: 8 servings

Cool-Rising Whole Wheat Bread

$3^{1}/_{2}$ to $4^{1}/_{2}$ cups all-purpose flour
3 envelopes dry yeast
1 tablespoon salt
$^{1}/_{2}$ cup honey
3 tablespoons butter or margarine, softened
$2^{1}/_{2}$ cups very warm water (120 to 130 degrees)
$2^{1}/_{2}$ cups whole wheat flour
Vegetable oil

Combine 2 cups of the all-purpose flour, yeast and salt in a large mixer bowl, blending well. Stir in the honey and butter.

Add the warm water. Beat at medium speed for 2 minutes. Add 1 cup of the all-purpose flour and $^{1}/_{2}$ cup of the whole wheat flour. Beat until thick and elastic, scraping down the side of the bowl occasionally. Stir in the remaining 2 cups whole wheat flour. Add enough of the remaining all-purpose flour to make a soft dough that leaves the side of the bowl.

Shape the dough into a ball on a lightly floured surface. Knead for 5 to 10 minutes or until smooth and elastic. Cover with greased waxed paper and a towel. Let rest for 20 minutes.

Punch down the dough and divide into halves. Shape each half into a loaf. Place in 2 greased 4x8-inch loaf pans. Brush the tops with oil. Cover loosely with greased waxed paper or plastic wrap.

Refrigerate for 2 to 24 hours. Let stand at room temperature for 10 minutes before baking. Puncture any surface bubbles with a wooden pick.

Bake at 400 degrees on lower oven rack for 30 to 35 minutes. Remove from the pans. The loaves are done if the bottoms sound hollow when tapped. Cool the loaves on their sides on wire racks.

Yield: 24 servings

A Mixture of Fall

In 1963, the Junior League of Parkersburg hosted the first annual Harvest Moon Festival, an area arts and crafts fair held every September at the City Park. Crowds gather annually from all around the state and surrounding states to buy the wares from the many talented artists and craftsmen that exhibit each year.

The following is the original Sloppy Joe recipe that the League members prepared and sold at the concession stand as a fundraiser during the first year. It was submitted by Mrs. Van L. Hall, Sustainer.

Harvest Moon Sloppy Joe Sauce

4 (14-ounce) bottles catsup
1/2 cup vinegar
1/2 cup prepared mustard
1/2 cup Worcestershire sauce
1/4 cup sugar
1 teaspoon salt
1 teaspoon pepper
8 pounds ground beef
1/8 teaspoon celery seeds

Combine the catsup, vinegar, mustard, Worcestershire sauce, sugar, salt and pepper in a saucepan. Bring to a boil; reduce the heat to low. Simmer for 15 minutes.

Brown the ground beef with the celery seeds in a Dutch oven, stirring until the ground beef is crumbly; drain. Stir in the catsup mixture. Simmer for 15 minutes.

Yield: 48 servings

Easy No-Knead Pizza Crust

$1/2$ cup warm water (105 to
    115 degrees)
1 envelope dry yeast
2 teaspoons sugar
1 tablespoon vegetable oil
$1/2$ teaspoon salt
$1^1/2$ cups (about) flour

Combine the water and yeast in a bowl; stir to dissolve the yeast. Stir in the sugar. Let stand at room temperature until foamy. Add the oil and salt and mix well. Add the flour $1/4$ cup at a time, mixing well after each addition. Add enough flour to form a stiff dough that is not sticky. Place the dough in an oiled bowl. Cover with a damp towel and let rise in a warm place for at least 10 minutes.

Punch down the dough. Press onto a greased 14-inch pizza pan. Top as desired.

Bake at 425 degrees for 15 minutes.

Note: May also use this dough to make breadsticks.

Yield: 1 pizza crust

Pepperoni and Cheese Loaf

1 loaf frozen bread dough,
   thawed
1 egg, beaten
$1/2$ cup grated Parmesan cheese
8 ounces sliced pepperoni
2 cups shredded mozzarella
   cheese
$1/2$ teaspoon oregano

Let the bread dough rise according to the package directions.

Punch down the dough. Turn onto a lightly floured surface. Roll into a large circle. Combine the egg and Parmesan cheese in a bowl, mixing well. Spread the egg mixture over the dough to within $1/2$ inch of the edge. Top with the pepperoni and mozzarella cheese. Sprinkle with the oregano.

Roll up the dough jelly roll style. Pinch the seam to seal and fold the ends under. Place seam side down on a baking sheet.

Bake at 375 degrees for 30 minutes. Cut into slices to serve.

Yield: 6 to 8 servings

Stromboli

2 cups bread flour
3/4 cup water
1 tablespoon butter or
   margarine
1 1/2 teaspoons dry yeast
1 teaspoon sugar
1 teaspoon coarsely ground
   pepper
1/2 teaspoon salt
1/4 cup shredded mozzarella
   cheese
1/4 cup shredded provolone
   cheese
1/4 cup shredded Gouda cheese
4 ounces sliced ham
4 ounces sliced capocollo
Olive oil

Place the flour, water, butter, yeast, sugar, pepper and salt into a bread machine according to the manufacturer's directions. Mix into a dough.

Remove the dough from the bread machine and divide into halves. Roll each half into a rectangle on a lightly floured surface. Cover the center third of each rectangle with half the mozzarella, provolone, Gouda, ham and capocollo. Fold both sides of the dough over the filling. Pinch the ends to seal. Place seam side down on a lightly greased baking sheet. Cover and let rise for 30 minutes. Brush the top of the stromboli lightly with olive oil.

Bake at 350 degrees for 20 to 30 minutes or until golden brown.

Yield: 4 servings

Breakfast · Brunch

Breakfast · Brunch

Cheesy Scrambled Egg Casserole

1/4 cup chopped onion

1/4 cup chopped green
    bell pepper

3 tablespoons margarine or
    butter

2 cups cubed cooked ham

12 eggs, beaten

1 (4-ounce) jar sliced
    mushrooms, drained

1 (10-ounce) can Cheddar
    cheese soup

1/2 cup grated Parmesan cheese

1/4 cup seasoned dry bread
    crumbs

Sauté the onion and green pepper in the margarine in a large skillet until the onion is tender-crisp. Add the ham and eggs. Cook over medium heat until the eggs are firm but moist, stirring occasionally. Remove from the heat. Fold in the mushrooms.

Combine the soup and 1/4 cup of the Parmesan cheese in a small bowl, mixing well. Gently fold into the egg mixture. Spoon into a greased 8x12-inch baking dish. Sprinkle with the bread crumbs and remaining 1/4 cup Parmesan cheese.

Bake at 350 degrees for 25 to 30 minutes or until golden brown.

Note: May assemble the night before, cover and refrigerate. In the morning, uncover and bake at 350 degrees for 35 minutes.

Yield: 12 servings

Sausage Breakfast Casserole

6 slices bread, crusts trimmed
Butter or margarine, softened
1 pound bulk pork sausage
1 1/2 cups shredded longhorn
  cheese
6 eggs, beaten
2 cups half-and-half
1 teaspoon salt

Spread the bread slices with desired amount of butter. Place in a greased 9x13-inch baking dish; set aside.

Brown the sausage in a skillet, stirring until crumbly; drain well. Spoon the sausage over the bread slices. Sprinkle with the cheese.

Combine the eggs, half-and-half and salt in a bowl, mixing well. Pour over the cheese. Refrigerate, covered, 8 hours or overnight. Remove from the refrigerator 15 minutes before baking.

Bake at 350 degrees for 45 minutes or until a knife inserted in the center comes out clean.

Yield: 8 servings

Crispy Bacon and Cheese Breakfast Casserole

2 cups garlic and onion
  croutons
1 cup shredded Cheddar cheese
2 cups milk
4 eggs
4 slices bacon, crisp-cooked,
  crumbled
1/2 teaspoon dry mustard
1/8 teaspoon onion powder
Salt and pepper to taste

Combine the croutons and cheese in an 8-inch square baking dish; mix well.

Beat the milk, eggs, bacon, dry mustard, onion powder, salt and pepper in a bowl. Pour over the cheese and croutons.

Bake at 350 degrees for 45 minutes.

Yield: 6 servings

Zucchini and Ham Quiche

2 cups shredded zucchini
1 cup baking mix
1 medium onion, chopped
1/2 cup diced ham
1/2 cup grated Romano cheese
1/2 cup olive oil
4 eggs
1 garlic cloves, crushed
1/2 teaspoon parsley flakes
1/2 teaspoon salt
1/2 teaspoon pepper
1/4 teaspoon oregano

Combine the zucchini, baking mix, onion, ham, Romano cheese, oil, eggs, garlic, parsley, salt, pepper and oregano in a large bowl, mixing well. Pour into a greased 9- or 10-inch quiche dish.

Bake at 350 degrees for 30 minutes or until a knife inserted in the center comes out clean.

Yield: 6 servings

Cheesy Hash Brown Potatoes

1 (32-ounce) package frozen
  hash brown potatoes, thawed
12 ounces sour cream
1 (10-ounce) can cream of
  celery soup
$1/2$ cup melted margarine
$1/2$ cup diced onion
1 teaspoon salt
$1/4$ teaspoon pepper
2 cups cornflakes
10 ounces shredded Cheddar
  cheese

Combine the potatoes, sour cream, soup, margarine, onion, salt and pepper in a bowl, mixing well. Spoon into a 9x13-inch baking pan. Sprinkle with the cornflakes. Top with the cheese.

Bake, covered, at 350 degrees for 30 minutes. Uncover. Bake for 15 minutes longer.

Yield: 20 servings

58

A Hint of Understanding

Beginning in 1987, the Junior League of Parkersburg sought to educate the public on the importance of organ donation. This was accomplished with a presentation that included a slide show. The League also provided public service announcements to local radio and television stations.

Filled Kolachke

1 cup unsalted butter, softened
6 ounces cream cheese,
  softened
2 cups sifted flour
1 tablespoon sugar
2 teaspoons baking powder
Apricot or strawberry preserves

Beat the butter and cream cheese in a mixer bowl until well blended. Sift the flour, sugar and baking powder together. Add to the cream cheese mixture. Stir and knead until well mixed. Refrigerate, covered, for 8 to 10 hours.

Roll out the dough on a lightly floured surface to a $^1/_8$-inch thickness. Cut into 2-inch x 3-inch rectangles. Spoon some preserves in the center of each rectangle. Bring 2 opposite corners together and pinch gently to seal. Sprinkle with additional sugar.

Bake at 350 degrees for 15 minutes or until golden brown.

Yield: about 3 dozen

Kaffekuchen

1/4 cup warm water (105 to
    115 degrees)
1 envelope dry yeast
1 cup vegetable shortening,
    at room temperature
2 cups sugar
1 cup milk, warmed
2 eggs
1 teaspoon salt
1 teaspoon lemon juice
1 teaspoon grated lemon zest
1 teaspoon vanilla extract
3 cups (about) sifted flour
1 cup sugar
1 cup flour
1 tablespoon cinnamon
1/2 cup butter

Combine the water and yeast in a small bowl; stir to dissolve the yeast. Cream the shortening and sugar. Add the milk, eggs, salt, lemon juice, lemon zest and vanilla and mix well. Add yeast mixture. Add enough of the sifted flour to make a stiff batter. Spread in a greased 9x13-inch baking pan. Cover and let rise until doubled.

Bake at 350 degrees for 30 minutes or until golden brown.

Combine 1 cup sugar, 1 cup flour, cinnamon and butter in a bowl, mixing until crumbly. Sprinkle over the top of the cake. Bake for 10 minutes longer.

Yield: 12 servings

Sister's Favorite Coffee Cake

1 (2-layer) package yellow cake
  mix
1 (4-ounce) package vanilla
  instant pudding mix
3 eggs
1 cup nonfat plain yogurt
1/4 cup vegetable oil
Sugar
Cinnamon

Beat the cake mix, pudding mix, eggs, yogurt and oil in a mixer bowl for 8 minutes. Pour half the batter into a greased and floured bundt pan.

Combine desired amounts of sugar and cinnamon in a bowl to make a cinnamon-sugar mixture. Sprinkle half over the batter in the pan. Top with the remaining batter. Sprinkle with the remaining cinnamon-sugar mixture. Swirl through the layers with a knife.

Bake at 350 degrees for 55 to 60 minutes or until a wooden pick inserted in the center of the cake comes out clean. Cool in the pan for 10 to 15 minutes. Remove from the pan and cool on a wire rack.

Note: May add brown sugar and chopped walnuts to the cinnamon-sugar mixture.

Yield: 16 servings

Twin Mountain Blueberry Coffee Cakes

2 cups flour
1 cup sugar
1 tablespoon baking powder
$^1/_4$ teaspoon salt
$^1/_2$ cup shortening
1 cup milk
2 eggs, beaten
$1^1/_2$ cups blueberries
$1^1/_4$ cups flaked coconut
Brown sugar to taste

Combine the flour, sugar, baking powder and salt in a large bowl; mix well. Cut in the shortening until the mixture resembles coarse crumbs.

Combine the milk and eggs in a bowl; mix well. Stir into the flour mixture. Fold in the blueberries. Pour the batter into 2 greased 9-inch round cake pans. Sprinkle with the coconut and a small amount of brown sugar.

Bake at 375 degrees for 25 minutes.

Note: May be cut in half to make 1 cake.

Yield: 12 servings

A Cup of Children's Theatre

The Children's Theatre began in 1929. Productions included Hansel and Gretel, Jack and the Beanstalk, Pinocchio, and many others. Children from all area schools were transported via the League to the productions. Three to four performances were staged each year. Tickets were sold to area children and given away to the Salvation Army, Union Mission, and Henry Logan Children's Home.

In later years, the League sponsored Lollipop concerts and a Children's Television series.

Banana Wheat Breakfast Muffins

4 bananas, cut into chunks
2 cups wheat bran cereal
1 cup milk
1 egg
2 egg whites
$1/4$ cup vegetable oil
$1^1/2$ cups flour
1 cup raisins
$1/2$ cup packed brown sugar
1 tablespoon baking powder
1 teaspoon baking soda
$2^1/2$ teaspoons cinnamon

Process the bananas in a blender or food processor container until puréed. Pour into a large bowl. Stir in the cereal; let stand until the cereal is soft.

Combine the milk, egg and egg whites in a separate bowl; mix well. Add to the banana mixture and mix well. Combine the flour, raisins, brown sugar, baking powder, baking soda and cinnamon in a bowl; mix well. Stir into the banana mixture, blending well. Fill 12 greased muffin cups $2/3$ full.

Bake at 400 degrees for 20 minutes.

Yield: 12 muffins

Blueberry Muffins

2 cups flour
1 cup sugar
2 teaspoons baking powder
1/2 teaspoon salt
1/2 cup butter
1/2 cup milk
2 eggs
1 teaspoon vanilla extract
2 1/2 cups blueberries

Combine the flour, sugar, baking powder and salt in a medium bowl; mix well. Cut in the butter with a pastry blender or 2 knives until the mixture resembles coarse crumbs.

Combine the milk, eggs and vanilla in a separate bowl; mix well. Add to the flour mixture and stir just until moistened. Do not overmix.

Crush 1/2 cup of the blueberries in a bowl. Stir into the muffin batter. Fold in the remaining 2 cups blueberries. Fill 12 greased muffin cups 2/3 full. Sprinkle additional sugar over the tops.

Bake at 375 degrees for 30 minutes or until a wooden pick inserted in the center comes out clean. Cool in the pans for 5 minutes. Remove to a wire rack.

Yield: 12 muffins

A Serving of Compassion

Being ever concerned about the welfare of children, especially underprivileged children, it was only natural that the Junior League of Parkersburg became involved with the local orphanage, the Henry Logan Children's Home.

Over the years, the League provided both financial assistance and volunteer time to improve the quality of life for these special children. From renovating and redecorating the home to providing Christmas presents for the children and funding summer camp and scouting programs, the members of the Junior League of Parkersburg touched the lives of some very needy children.

Raspberry Cheesecake Muffins

3 ounces cream cheese,
  softened
$1/3$ cup sugar
1 egg
$1/2$ teaspoon vanilla extract
1 cup milk
6 tablespoons butter
1 teaspoon vanilla extract
2 eggs
2 cups flour
$3/4$ cup sugar
$2^{1}/2$ teaspoons baking powder
$1/2$ teaspoon salt
1 cup fresh or frozen
  raspberries

Combine the cream cheese, $1/3$ cup sugar, 1 egg and $1/2$ teaspoon vanilla in a bowl, mixing well; set aside.

Combine the milk, butter and 1 teaspoon vanilla in a saucepan. Heat over low heat until the butter melts, stirring constantly. Remove from the heat and cool to lukewarm. Beat in 2 eggs.

Combine the flour, $3/4$ cup sugar, baking powder and salt in a bowl, mixing well. Add the milk mixture and stir just until mixed. Fold in the raspberries. Fill 12 greased or paper-lined muffin cups $2/3$ full. Top each muffin with 2 teaspoons of the cream cheese mixture and swirl slightly with a knife.

Bake at 400 degrees for 20 minutes or until the tops spring back when lightly touched.

Yield: 12 muffins

Try

Raisin Bran Muffins

5 cups flour
3 cups sugar
4 teaspoons baking soda
2 teaspoons salt
1 quart buttermilk
1 cup vegetable oil
4 eggs, beaten
1 (15-ounce) box Raisin
  Bran cereal

Combine the flour, sugar, baking soda and salt in a bowl; mix well. Add the buttermilk, oil and eggs and mix well. Stir in the cereal.

Refrigerate, covered, until ready to use. (Batter may be refrigerated for up to 6 to 8 weeks.) Fill desired number of greased muffin cups 2/3 full.

Bake at 425 degrees for 15 to 20 minutes or until a wooden pick inserted in the center comes out clean.

Yield: about 60 muffins

A Sprinkling of the Arts to Taste

The Junior League of Parkersburg established the Fine Arts Center in 1938. Through the years, the League was able to provide both amateur and professional artists of all ages. The Center provided a vehicle of exposure and education in various fields of artist talent.

Art programs and classes benefited many children of the Mid-Ohio Valley from kindergarten through grade twelve. The Fine Arts Center committee also hosted many regional exhibits and shows to enhance the Parkersburg community.

Hungarian Crêpes

1 cup sifted flour
2 tablespoons sugar
1/4 teaspoon salt
2 eggs, lightly beaten
1 cup milk
2 tablespoons melted butter or
   margarine
Vegetable oil
Butter
16 ounces cottage cheese
1 egg, beaten
Freshly chopped dill

Sift the flour, sugar and salt into a bowl. Add 2 eggs, milk and butter; beat until smooth.

Heat 1 tablespoon oil in a small skillet over medium-low heat until hot. Add about 1/4 cup batter, tilting the pan to spread the batter evenly over the bottom. Cook until lightly browned on the bottom; turn over. Cook the other side just until set. Do not overcook. Remove from the pan to a plate. Rub a small amount of butter over the top of the crêpe to prevent sticking. Repeat with the remaining batter, adding more oil to the skillet as needed and stacking the crêpes on the plate.

Combine the cottage cheese, 1 egg and dill in a bowl; mix well. Spoon down the center of the crêpes. Fold in the sides to enclose the filling. Place in a single layer in a shallow baking dish. Brush with melted butter.

Bake, covered, at 350 degrees for about 20 minutes or until heated through.

Yield: about 10 crêpes

Apple-Filled Oven French Toast

1 (12-ounce) loaf French bread
1 (21-ounce) can apple pie
   filling
8 eggs
2 cups milk
2 cups half-and-half
2 teaspoons vanilla extract
1/2 teaspoon nutmeg
1/2 teaspoon cinnamon
1 cup packed brown sugar
1 cup coarsely chopped pecans
1/2 cup butter, softened
2 tablespoons dark corn syrup

Slice the bread into 1-inch slices. Arrange a single layer of bread slices in the bottom of a buttered 9x13-inch baking pan. Spread the pie filling over the bread. Top with another layer of bread slices.

Combine the eggs, milk, half-and-half, vanilla, nutmeg and cinnamon in a blender container and process until well mixed. Pour over the top of the bread. Refrigerate, covered, 8 to 10 hours or overnight.

Combine the brown sugar, pecans, butter and corn syrup in a bowl; mix well. Spread over the top of the bread mixture.

Bake at 350 degrees for 50 minutes or until puffed and golden brown.

Yield: 8 to 10 servings

Weekend Waffles

2 cups flour
1 tablespoon plus 1 teaspoon
   baking powder
1/4 teaspoon salt
3 eggs, separated
1 1/4 cups (about) milk
6 tablespoons melted butter,
   cooled

Sift the flour, baking powder and salt together in a mixing bowl.

Beat the egg yolks in a bowl until well blended. Add the milk and butter and mix well.

Beat the egg whites in a bowl until soft peaks form. Add the flour mixture to the milk mixture and beat well. Fold in the egg whites.

Pour 1 cup of the batter on a preheated waffle iron. Bake until the waffles are golden brown. Serve with butter and warm maple syrup.

Yield: 4 servings

Combine an Ounce of Awareness

Over the years, the Junior League of Parkersburg has undertaken a number of projects focusing on improving the lives of the handicapped citizens of the area.

In 1984, the Kids on the Block project was developed to promote handicap awareness among school-aged children in grades 2-5. A puppet show which included role-playing activities, developed by the League members, traveled to the elementary schools to educate children about mentally and physically handicapped individuals in an attempt to promote acceptance.

After several very successful years, the project was turned over to the special education department of the Wood County Board of Education.

Hot Fruit Bake

1 (20-ounce) can pineapple slices, drained
1 (17-ounce) can apricot halves, drained
1 (16-ounce) can peach halves, drained
1 (16-ounce) can pear halves, drained
1 (15-ounce) jar spiced apple rings, drained
1/2 cup butter or margarine
1/2 cup sugar
2 tablespoons cornstarch
1 cup dry sherry

Layer the pineapple, apricots, peaches, pears and apples in a 2-quart baking dish.

Melt the butter in a small saucepan. Combine the sugar and cornstarch in a bowl; stir into the butter. Add the sherry gradually, stirring constantly. Cook over low heat until thickened and smooth, stirring constantly. Pour over the fruit.

Refrigerate, covered, for 8 to 10 hours or overnight. Remove the baking dish from the refrigerator 15 minutes before baking.

Bake, uncovered, at 350 degrees for 30 minutes or until bubbly.

Yield: 10 servings

Pineapple Scallop

6 slices bread, lightly toasted
1 (15-ounce) can pineapple tidbits
1 cup sugar
1/2 cup melted margarine
1/3 cup half-and-half, milk or evaporated milk
2 eggs, beaten
Brown sugar to taste
Cinnamon to taste

Cut the toasted bread into cubes. Combine the bread cubes, undrained pineapple, sugar, margarine, half-and-half and eggs in a bowl; mix well. Spoon into a 2-quart baking dish. Sprinkle with brown sugar and cinnamon.

Bake at 350 degrees for 45 minutes. Serve warm.

Note: May serve with ice cream or whipped cream for dessert.

Yield: 6 servings

Soups

Soups

Champagne Melon Peach Soup

1 ripe cantaloupe, peeled,
   seeded
2½ pounds fresh peaches,
   peeled, pitted
¼ bottle Champagne

Cut the cantaloupe and peaches into chunks. Purée in a blender or food processor. Pour into a bowl and stir to blend. Refrigerate, covered, until chilled.

Fill Champagne glasses ⅔ full with fruit purée. Top with Champagne. Garnish with fresh mint sprigs.

Note: This makes a lovely addition to a brunch menu.

Yield: 6 servings

Carrot and Orange Soup

2 cups chopped yellow onions
$1/4$ cup unsalted butter
4 to 7 cups chicken stock
12 large carrots, peeled,
   chopped ($1^1/2$ to 2 pounds)
1 cup freshly squeezed
   orange juice
Salt and pepper to taste
Grated orange zest to taste

Sauté the onions in the butter in a large saucepan over low heat for 25 minutes or until lightly browned.

Add 4 cups of the stock and the carrots. Bring to a boil; reduce the heat to low. Simmer, covered, for 30 minutes or until the carrots are tender.

Strain the mixture, reserving the stock. Purée the vegetables with 1 cup of the stock in a blender or food processor container. Return the stock and vegetable purée to the saucepan.

Stir in the orange juice and enough of the remaining stock to reach the desired consistency. Season with salt, pepper and orange zest. Simmer until heated through. Serve immediately.

Yield: 4 to 6 servings

Carolina Black Bean Soup

1 cup chopped onion
1 cup chopped green bell
 pepper
1 tablespoon olive oil
3 (15-ounce) cans black beans
3 (8-ounce) cans tomato sauce
1 garlic clove, pressed
1 teaspoon salt
1 teaspoon pepper

Sauté the onion and green pepper in the oil in a skillet until tender.

Transfer to a slow cooker. Add the undrained black beans, tomato sauce, garlic, salt and pepper. Cook, covered, on Low for 2 to 3 hours. Serve with corn bread, sausage or chicken.

Yield: 6 to 8 servings

Broccoli Onion and Cheese Soup

2 (10-ounce) packages frozen
 chopped broccoli
1 tablespoon instant minced
 onion
1 (10-ounce) can cream of
 mushroom soup
1 1/2 cups milk
2 tablespoons butter or
 margarine
8 ounces Velveeta cheese, cut
 into chunks

Cook the broccoli with the onion in a large saucepan according to the broccoli package directions. Stir in the soup, milk and butter near the end of the cooking time. Return to a boil; reduce the heat to low. Simmer for 2 to 3 minutes.

Add the cheese, stirring constantly, until completely melted.

Note: May substitute cream of chicken soup for the cream of mushroom soup.

Yield: 6 servings

Cream of Cauliflower Soup

2 cups chopped cauliflower
1 1/2 cups water
1/2 cup chopped onion
2 teaspoons instant chicken
   bouillon
3/4 teaspoon curry powder
2 tablespoons margarine
2 tablespoons flour
1/4 teaspoon salt
1/8 teaspoon pepper
1 cup milk

Combine the cauliflower, water, onion, instant bouillon and curry powder in a saucepan; mix well. Bring to a boil; reduce the heat to low. Simmer, covered, for 10 minutes. Pour into a large heatproof bowl.

Melt the margarine in the same saucepan. Blend in the flour, salt and pepper until smooth. Add the milk gradually, stirring constantly until the mixture is thickened and bubbly.

Stir in the cauliflower mixture. Cook until heated through, stirring constantly.

Yield: 4 servings

A Quart of Awareness

The Silent Witness Program began in 1996. This ongoing program is supported by the Junior League to honor women and children killed as a result of domestic violence, in addition to raising public awareness of this problem. The program also provides a means to connect victims with local resources and to encourage legislative action aimed at ending domestic violence. The national goal of the program is to end domestic violence by the year 2010.

The Junior League of Parkersburg has sponsored nationally known speakers to address the community and the League has also participated on the national level in its efforts to eliminate domestic violence by taking part in a national walk in Washington, DC.

Minestrone

3/4 cup chopped onion

2 garlic cloves, minced

3 tablespoons olive oil

8 cups boiling water

1 1/2 cups diced zucchini

1 1/2 cups coarsely chopped
   cabbage

1 cup diced potatoes

1 cup chick-peas or beans

1 (14-ounce) can tomatoes

1/4 cup chopped celery

2 teaspoons salt

1 teaspoon parsley

1/2 teaspoon basil

1/8 teaspoon pepper

1 cup cooked macaroni

Sauté the onion and garlic in the oil in a large stockpot until tender.

Add the water, zucchini, cabbage, potatoes, chick-peas, undrained tomatoes, celery, salt, parsley, basil and pepper. Simmer for about 1 1/2 hours or until the vegetables are tender.

Stir in the macaroni and heat through. Serve hot.

Note: For a heartier soup, may add 1 1/2 pounds browned beef or pork.

Yield: 6 to 8 servings

Light Potato Soup

3 cups water
3 potatoes, peeled, diced
1 onion, diced
1 1/2 teaspoons salt
1/2 teaspoon paprika
1/4 teaspoon pepper
1 cup chicken consommé
1 cup skim milk

Combine the water, potatoes, onion, salt, paprika and pepper in a saucepan; mix well. Bring to a boil; reduce the heat to low. Simmer, covered, for 35 minutes.

Purée the vegetables in a blender container. Return to the pan.

Add the consommé and milk. Heat over low heat for 15 minutes.

Yield: 6 servings

Rosie's Potato Soup

8 to 10 medium potatoes, peeled, diced
1 medium onion, diced
2 (10-ounce) cans cream of celery soup
3 soup cans milk
Salt and pepper to taste
2 tablespoons butter

Combine the potatoes and onion in a large saucepan with enough water to cover. Bring to a boil; reduce the heat to low. Simmer until the potatoes are tender; drain.

Add the soup, milk, salt and pepper. Mash potatoes slightly with a potato masher to thicken the soup.

Remove from the heat. Stir in the butter. Cook until heated through.

Yield: 8 servings

A Measure of Media

To raise community awareness, the media has proven to be a strong partner for this organization throughout the years. Beginning in 1937 with the sponsoring of a radio program and continuing to the airing of the League's first television series in 1955, the Junior League of Parkersburg has been at the forefront of technology when it comes to enriching the lives of the people in the community.

As a result, children were treated to a variety of radio and TV programs aimed at educating and enriching their lives. Adults weren't left out. Civic-minded programs like Let's Explore Parkersburg and Know Your Community were popular outlets of information.

Herbed Root Vegetable Soup

2 yellow onions, chopped
2 or 3 shallots, chopped
1 leek, trimmed, rinsed,
 thinly sliced
2 cloves of garlic, minced
5 tablespoons unsalted butter
3 potatoes, peeled
2 parsnips, peeled
2 carrots, peeled
2 turnips, peeled
1 large celery root, peeled
1 1/2 quarts chicken stock
Salt and pepper to taste

Cook the onions, shallots, leek and garlic in the butter in a large saucepan over low heat for 5 to 10 minutes or until tender but not brown.

Cut the potatoes, parsnips, carrots, turnips and celery root into 1/2-inch dice. Add to the onion mixture with the stock. Bring to a boil; reduce the heat to low. Simmer for 35 minutes or until the vegetables are tender.

Purée half the soup at a time in a food processor or blender container. Return to the pan. Simmer until heated through. Season with salt and pepper. Garnish with sprigs of fresh cilantro, parsley, chervil or watercress.

Yield: 4 to 6 servings

A Gallon of Laughter

The most recent undertaking of the Junior League of Parkersburg is the Children's Discovery Center, a $4 million, three-phase project, the goal of which is to develop a facility that will provide children, grades kindergarten through 6, with interactive, hands-on educational exhibits set in a fun atmosphere.

The project is currently in the design and fund-raising stage, and the Junior League and the community are hopeful that at least the first phase of the proposed 18,000-square-foot facility will be up and running within the next few years.

Red Pepper Soup

8 red bell peppers
3 carrots, peeled
1 pear, peeled
3 shallots
2 garlic cloves
$1/4$ cup unsalted butter
1 tablespoon olive oil
1 quart chicken stock
1 teaspoon crushed red pepper
$1/8$ teaspoon cayenne pepper
Salt and black pepper to taste

Roast 2 of the red peppers over a gas flame or under the broiler until charred on all sides. Place in a paper bag; close the bag. Let stand for 5 to 10 minutes to sweat. Remove the blackened skins under cold running water. Remove and discard the cores and seeds. Drain peppers on paper towels.

Slice the remaining 6 red peppers, carrots, pear, shallots and garlic. Sauté the vegetables and pear in the butter and oil in a large skillet over medium-low heat for 10 to 15 minutes or until tender.

Add the stock, crushed red pepper, cayenne pepper, salt and black pepper to the skillet. Bring to a boil; reduce the heat to low. Simmer, covered, for 25 to 30 minutes.

Purée the soup in a blender or food processor container, adding the 2 roasted red peppers. Return to the pan. Cook over low heat until heated through. Garnish with fresh tarragon.

Yield: 4 to 6 servings

Homemade Tomato Soup

2 carrots, chopped
2 ribs celery, chopped
1 onion, chopped
2 tablespoons butter
3 cups chicken broth
6 ripe tomatoes, peeled,
  chopped
2 tablespoons butter
1/4 cup sugar
Salt and pepper to taste
1 cup milk or cream

Sauté the carrots, celery and onion in 2 tablespoons butter in a saucepan until tender.

Add the broth. Bring to a boil; reduce the heat to low. Simmer for 20 minutes.

Sauté the tomatoes in 2 tablespoons butter in a skillet until tender. Add to the vegetables and broth. Simmer for 20 minutes. Stir in the sugar, salt and pepper.

Purée the soup in a food mill or blender container. Return to the pan. Add the milk. Cook over low heat until heated through, stirring constantly.

Yield: 6 to 8 servings

Two Cups of the Creative Arts

In 1984, a series of workshops in the areas of dance, drama, music, and art was presented to mentally challenged children ages eight to sixteen as an introduction to the arts. The Junior League of Parkersburg initially partnered with the Wood County Association for Retarded Citizens (ARC) on the project, and turned it over to the ARC after the series was up and running.

Vegetarian "Chicken" Soup

1 large onion, diced
3 garlic cloves, coarsely
  chopped
1 tablespoon olive oil
3/4 cup yellow split peas
1 teaspoon turmeric
4 quarts water
3 cups diced carrots
3 cups diced potatoes
1 medium onion, diced
1 green bell pepper, diced
1 cup diced celery
1 tablespoon dried cilantro
Freshly ground pepper to taste

Sauté the large onion and garlic in the oil in a large saucepan for 2 to 3 minutes. Add the split peas and turmeric. Sauté for 1 minute.

Add the water. Bring to a boil; reduce the heat to low. Simmer for 30 minutes or until the peas are tender. Purée the pea mixture in a blender container or using a hand mixer. Return to the pan.

Stir in the carrots, potatoes, medium onion, green pepper, celery, cilantro and pepper. Simmer gently for 30 minutes or until the vegetables are tender. Serve over rice or egg noodles.

Note: Great soup for vegetarians who miss the chicken soup mom used to make.

Yield: 12 servings

Vegetarian Three-Bean Chili

1 large onion, diced
1 green bell pepper, diced
12 ounces extra-firm tofu,
　diced (optional)
1 tablespoon olive oil
1 (28-ounce) can diced
　tomatoes
1 (28-ounce) can tomato sauce
1 (15-ounce) can kidney beans
1 (15-ounce) can great
　Northern beans
1 (15-ounce) can black beans
4 garlic cloves, minced
2 tablespoons tomato paste
1/4 cup chili powder or to taste
2 teaspoons oregano
1/4 teaspoon thyme
1/4 teaspoon freshly ground
　pepper, or to taste
1/8 teaspoon cumin

Sauté the onion, green pepper and tofu in the oil in a large saucepan for 4 to 5 minutes or until the vegetables are tender.

Add the tomatoes, tomato sauce, undrained kidney beans, undrained great Northern beans, undrained black beans, garlic, tomato paste, chili powder, oregano, thyme, pepper and cumin. Bring to a boil; reduce the heat to low.

Simmer, uncovered, for 45 minutes, stirring occasionally. Adjust the seasonings to taste. Serve over rice or egg noodles. Garnish with shredded cheese.

Note: Tofu, in addition to being an excellent source of soy protein, adds texture to the chili and absorbs the flavor of the other ingredients.

Yield: 12 servings

Winter White Chili

2 boneless skinless chicken
  breasts
1 medium onion, diced
1 rib celery, chopped (optional)
3 (15-ounce) cans navy beans
2 (14-ounce) cans chicken
  broth
1/2 cup water
1 (4-ounce) can chopped
  green chiles
1 garlic clove, pressed
1/2 teaspoon chili powder
1/2 teaspoon cumin (optional)
Salt and pepper to taste
1/2 cup fat-free sour cream

Spray a skillet with nonstick cooking spray. Sauté the chicken, onion and celery in the skillet until the chicken is cooked through; cool slightly.

Chop the chicken into small pieces. Place the chicken, onion, celery, undrained beans, broth, water, undrained chiles, garlic, chili powder, cumin, salt and pepper in a slow cooker. Cook, covered, on Low for 2 to 3 hours. Top each serving with about 1 tablespoon sour cream. Serve with corn bread.

Yield: 6 to 8 servings

All-In-One Beef Stew

1½ pounds beef or veal
    stew meat
6 carrots
4 ribs celery
2 large turnips or potatoes
½ pound mushrooms
1 (14-ounce) can stewed
    tomatoes
1 (10-ounce) can cream of
    onion soup
1 cup water
¼ cup dry white wine
⅓ cup quick-cooking tapioca
1 teaspoon salt
¼ teaspoon garlic powder
3 to 4 whole black peppercorns
1 bay leaf

Cut the beef, carrots and celery into 1-inch cubes. Cut the turnips and mushrooms into quarters and combine with the beef, carrots and celery in a large Dutch oven. Add the undrained tomatoes, cream of onion soup, water and wine; mix well. Stir in the tapioca, salt, garlic powder, peppercorns and bay leaf.

Bake, covered, at 350 degrees for 3 hours. Remove the peppercorns and bay leaf before serving.

Yield: 6 to 8 servings

Old-Fashioned Chicken Soup

1 (4- to 4^1/2-pound) chicken
3 quarts water
2 onions, peeled
6 whole cloves
3 carrots
3 ribs celery
3 leeks
^{1}/2 cup fresh parsley leaves
^{1}/2 teaspoon dillweed
3 carrots
3 ribs celery
Cooked noodles or rice
   (optional)

Wash chicken and remove any excess fat. Place the chicken and water in a stockpot. Stud the onions with the cloves; add to the pot. Bring to a boil; reduce the heat to low. Simmer, covered, for 1^1/2 hours.

Cut 3 carrots, 3 ribs celery and leeks into 2-inch pieces. Add to the pot with the parsley and dillweed. Simmer for 1 hour.

Remove the chicken from the pot. Strain the stock. Remove the meat from the chicken and cut into chunks. Skim off and discard any fat from the surface of the stock.

Return the stock and chicken meat to the pot. Slice 3 carrots and 3 ribs celery; add to the pot with noodles or rice. Simmer for 20 to 25 minutes or until the vegetables are tender.

Yield: 12 servings

Seafood Gazpacho

2 pounds tomatoes
1 large red bell pepper
1/2 medium cucumber, peeled
1 small rib celery
1 small onion
2 garlic cloves, minced
1 slice white bread, torn into
    small pieces
1 cup water
1/4 cup sherry vinegar or red
    wine vinegar
1/4 cup extra-virgin olive oil
1 teaspoon salt
1/8 teaspoon Tabasco sauce
1 pound mixed cooked seafood
    (see note)
1/2 medium cucumber, peeled,
    seeded, diced
1 small yellow or green bell
    pepper, diced
2 tablespoons chopped fresh
    cilantro leaves

Coarsely chop the tomatoes, red pepper and one 1/2 cucumber, discarding any seeds. Chop the celery and onion and combine with the tomatoes, red pepper and coarsely chopped cucumber in a large bowl. Add the garlic, bread, water, vinegar, olive oil, salt and Tabasco sauce; mix well. Refrigerate, covered, for at least 1 hour, making sure the bread is completely immersed.

Purée the tomato mixture in a blender until very smooth. Strain into a bowl to remove any seeds or skin. Refrigerate, covered, until thoroughly chilled. Taste and adjust the seasonings.

Ladle the soup into cold serving bowls. Top with the seafood, diced cucumber, yellow pepper and cilantro.

Note: For the seafood, a combination of crab meat, shrimp, scallops or mussels would work well in this dish. If fresh tomatoes are not juicy and flavorful, substitute good-quality canned tomatoes.

Yield: 8 servings

Compliments of the Greenbrier Hotel

Salads

Salads

Taffy Apple Salad

1 (8-ounce) can crushed
   pineapple
$^1/_2$ cup sugar
1 egg, beaten
1 tablespoon flour
2 tablespoons apple cider
   vinegar
8 ounces whipped topping
5 Granny Smith apples,
   chopped
1 cup chopped peanuts

Combine the undrained pineapple, sugar, egg, flour and vinegar in a saucepan; mix well. Cook over medium heat until thickened. Refrigerate until cooled.

Spoon the whipped topping into a large bowl. Fold in the pineapple mixture. Add the apples and $^3/4$ cup of the peanuts. Toss until well blended. Top with the remaining $^1/4$ cup peanuts. Refrigerate, covered, until ready to serve.

Yield: 12 servings

A Pinch of History

A local historical landmark, the Blennerhassett Mansion, had deteriorated to the point where it was no longer being utilized by the community as an educational tool or to entice tourism.

In 1987, the Junior League embarked on a research project which included gathering information regarding various aspects, such as interior architectural design, furnishings, educational outreach opportunities, and fund-raising ideas.

The following two years saw the League completing a video depicting the story of the Blennerhassett's lives in the Mid-Ohio Valley for the Blennerhassett Historical Commission. The League also did more research on the Mansion's library and laboratory.

Try

Winter Apple Walnut Salad

4 cups diced apples
1 (20-ounce) can pineapple
  chunks, drained
3/4 cup chopped walnuts
1 cup orange juice
1/2 cup sugar
1 tablespoon flour
1 cup miniature marshmallows

Combine the apples, pineapple and walnuts in a bowl; mix well and set aside.

Blend the orange juice, sugar and flour in a small saucepan. Cook over low heat until smooth and thickened, stirring constantly.

Pour the hot orange juice mixture over the fruit mixture and mix well. Refrigerate until chilled. Stir in the marshmallows just before serving.

Yield: 6 servings

Cranberry Waldorf Delight

1 (12-ounce) package fresh
  cranberries
1 (16-ounce) package
  miniature marshmallows
1/2 cup sugar
1 large apple, peeled, chopped
1 cup red seedless grapes, cut
  into halves
1/2 cup chopped walnuts
1/2 pint whipping cream
1 teaspoon vanilla extract or
  Grand Marnier

Wash the cranberries, discarding any that are soft. Finely chop the cranberries or grind in a blender or food processor container. Transfer to a bowl. Add the marshmallows and sugar and mix well. Refrigerate, covered, for 8 to 10 hours.

Fold the apple, grapes and walnuts into the cranberry mixture; set aside.

Beat the cream with the vanilla in a chilled bowl with chilled beaters until soft peaks form. Fold the whipped cream into the fruit mixture. Refrigerate, covered, until ready to serve.

Yield: 10 servings

Cranberry Soufflé Salad

1 envelope unflavored gelatin
1 cup water
2 tablespoons sugar
1/4 teaspoon salt
1/2 cup mayonnaise
2 tablespoons lemon juice
1 teaspoon grated lemon zest
1 (16-ounce) can whole
    cranberry sauce
1 apple, peeled and diced, or
    1 (8-ounce) can pineapple
    tidbits, drained
1/4 cup chopped walnuts

Soften the gelatin in 1/4 cup of the water in a small saucepan. Stir in the remaining 3/4 cup water, sugar and salt. Cook over low heat until the gelatin is completely dissolved, stirring constantly. Remove from the heat. Pour into mixer bowl.

Beat in the mayonnaise, lemon juice and lemon zest until well blended. Place in the freezer for 10 to 15 minutes or until the mixture is firm 1 inch from the edge and the center is soft.

Beat until fluffy. Fold in the cranberry sauce, apple and walnuts 1 at a time. Pour into a greased 2-quart mold. Refrigerate, covered, until firm.

Unmold onto a serving plate garnished with greens and fresh cranberries.

Yield: 6 to 8 servings

Mandarin Orange and Almond Salad

1/4 cup vegetable oil

2 tablespoons sugar

2 tablespoons vinegar

1 tablespoon snipped parsley

1/2 teaspoon salt

1/8 teaspoon black pepper

1/8 teaspoon red pepper sauce

1/4 cup sliced almonds

1 tablespoon plus 1 teaspoon
   sugar

1/4 head lettuce

1/4 head romaine lettuce

2 green onions, thinly sliced
   (optional)

8 ounces bacon, crisp-cooked,
   crumbled (optional)

1 (11-ounce) can mandarin
   oranges, drained

Place the oil, 2 tablespoons sugar, vinegar, parsley, salt, black pepper and red pepper sauce in a jar; cover tightly. Shake to combine. Refrigerate until chilled.

Cook the almonds with 1 tablespoon plus 1 teaspoon sugar in a skillet over low heat until the almonds are warm and coated with the sugar; cool. Break apart and set aside.

Tear the lettuces into bite-size pieces. Combine the lettuce and onions in a bowl; mix well. Pour the chilled dressing over the lettuce mixture 5 minutes before serving; toss well. Add the almonds, bacon and oranges and toss gently. Serve immediately.

Yield: 4 servings

Pineapple Delight Salad

1 cup crushed pineapple with
    juice
8 ounces marshmallows
6 ounces cream cheese,
    softened
1/4 cup mayonnaise
1/2 pint whipping cream,
    whipped

Drain the pineapple, reserving the juice in a bowl. Cut up the marshmallows and add to the pineapple juice. Let soak until soft and all the juice is absorbed. (If any juice remains, drain and discard.)

Beat the cream cheese and mayonnaise in a mixer bowl. Stir in the pineapple and marshmallows. Fold in the whipped cream. Refrigerate, covered, until ready to serve.

Yield: 6 servings

Strawberry Pretzel Salad

2 cups crushed pretzels
3/4 cup melted butter
1/4 cup sugar
8 ounces whipped topping
8 ounces cream cheese,
    softened
1 cup sugar
1 (6-ounce) package strawberry
    gelatin
2 cups boiling water
1 (20-ounce) package frozen
    strawberries

Combine the pretzels, butter and 1/4 cup sugar in a bowl; mix well. Spread over the bottom of a 9x13-inch baking pan. Bake at 400 degrees for 6 minutes; cool completely.

Combine the whipped topping, cream cheese and 1 cup sugar in a bowl; mix well. Spread over the cooled pretzel crust.

Dissolve the gelatin in the boiling water in a bowl. Stir in the frozen strawberries. Refrigerate until almost set. Spread over the cream cheese layer. Refrigerate, covered, until set.

Yield: 12 servings

Summer Picnic Fruit Salad

1 (21-ounce) can peach pie filling
1 (20-ounce) can pineapple chunks, drained
1 (11-ounce) can mandarin oranges, drained
1 (10-ounce) package frozen sliced strawberries, thawed, drained
$1/2$ to 1 cup chopped pecans (optional)
2 medium bananas, sliced

Combine the peach pie filling, pineapple, oranges, strawberries and pecans in a large serving bowl; mix well. Refrigerate, covered, for 8 to 12 hours.

Stir in the banana slices just before serving.

Yield: 15 servings

Italian Pasta Salad

1 pound bow tie pasta, cooked
12 ounces pepperoni, sliced
8 ounces salami, diced
8 ounces provolone cheese, diced
1 (6-ounce) can pitted black olives, drained
3 medium tomatoes, diced
2 medium green bell peppers, diced
$2/3$ cup olive oil
$1/2$ cup vinegar
1 teaspoon pepper
$1/2$ teaspoon salt

Combine the pasta, pepperoni, salami, provolone cheese, olives, tomatoes and green peppers in a bowl.

Mix the oil, vinegar, pepper and salt in a small bowl until well blended. Pour over the pasta mixture and toss to coat well. Refrigerate, covered, for 8 to 10 hours.

Yield: 8 servings

try

Marinated Antipasto Salad

1 pound medium pasta shells,
   cooked
1 (6-ounce) can pitted black
   olives, drained, sliced
8 ounces hard salami, sliced
8 to 12 ounces provolone
   cheese, cut into small cubes
4 ounces pepperoni, sliced
3 small tomatoes,
   cut into wedges
2 green bell peppers,
   cut into strips
2 ribs celery, sliced
3/4 cup vegetable oil
1/2 cup red wine vinegar
1 to 1 1/4 tablespoons oregano
1 tablespoon salt
1 teaspoon pepper

Combine the pasta shells, olives, salami, provolone cheese, pepperoni, tomatoes, green peppers and celery in a 9x13-inch baking dish.

Mix the oil, vinegar, oregano, salt and pepper in a bowl until well blended. Pour over the pasta mixture and toss to coat well. Refrigerate, covered, for 8 to 10 hours, stirring occasionally.

Yield: 12 servings

Roasted Pecan Chicken Salad

4 cups cubed cooked chicken
   breasts
4 cups diced celery
2 cups pecans, roasted and
   salted
1¹/₂ cups Mayonnaise (below)
¹/₂ cup Boiled Dressing
   (page 99)

Combine the chicken, celery and pecans in a bowl; mix well.

Blend the mayonnaise and boiled dressing in a bowl. Add to the chicken mixture and toss gently.

Yield: 12 servings

Mayonnaise

4 teaspoons lemon juice
4 teaspoons apple cider vinegar
1 tablespoon tarragon vinegar
1 tablespoon sugar
1 teaspoon salt
1 teaspoon paprika
1 teaspoon dry mustard
1 teaspoon Worcestershire
   sauce
¹/₈ teaspoon white pepper
Drop of Tabasco sauce
¹/₃ cup egg yolks
3¹/₃ cups vegetable oil

Combine the lemon juice, cider vinegar, tarragon vinegar, sugar, salt, paprika, dry mustard, Worcestershire sauce, white pepper and Tabasco sauce in a bowl; mix well.

Beat the egg yolks in a bowl until light and creamy. Add the vinegar mixture and oil alternately to the egg yolks gradually, beating constantly. Beat until thick and creamy.

Yield: 1 quart

Boiled Dressing

1/2 cup flour
1/2 cup sugar
1 tablespoon salt
2 teaspoons dry mustard
1 teaspoon paprika
2 cups milk
1 cup vinegar
3 egg yolks

Mix the flour, sugar, salt, dry mustard and paprika in the top of a double boiler. Add the milk gradually, stirring until smooth. Place over simmering water. Heat until thickened, stirring frequently.

Heat the vinegar in a saucepan until hot. Add to the milk mixture. Cook for 10 minutes.

Beat the egg yolks in a bowl. Add a small amount of the hot milk mixture gradually to the egg yolks, stirring constantly. Stir the egg yolk mixture gradually into the remaining milk mixture. Cook for 10 minutes. Refrigerate, covered, until chilled.

Yield: 1 quart

Delightful Chicken Salad

1 (2-ounce) package slivered almonds
1/2 tablespoon butter
10 chicken breasts, cooked and chopped
2 cups cooked long grain rice
2 cups diced celery
2 cups green grape halves
2 cups mayonnaise
2 cups ranch salad dressing
2 (11-ounce) cans mandarin oranges, drained
2 tablespoons chopped onion

Sauté the almonds in the butter in a skillet until golden brown; drain on paper towels.

Combine the chicken, rice, celery, grapes, mayonnaise, salad dressing, oranges and onion in a bowl, mixing gently. Top with the almonds. Refrigerate, covered, for 2 hours.

Yield: 15 to 20 servings

Tuna on Tuesday Bridge Club Salad

4 (6-ounce) cans white tuna
2 (6-ounce) packages long grain
  and wild rice
1 cup chopped celery
1 cup cashews, chopped
1 cup sour cream
1 cup mayonnaise
1/2 cup chopped green onions
Juice of 1/2 lemon

Rinse the tuna under hot water; drain.

Prepare the rice according to the package directions; cool slightly.

Combine the tuna, cooked rice, celery, cashews, sour cream, mayonnaise, green onions and lemon juice in a bowl; mix well. Refrigerate, covered, until chilled. Serve on a bed of lettuce.

Yield: 8 servings

Zesty Shrimp and Artichoke Hearts

3/4 cup vegetable oil
1/4 cup red wine vinegar
1 egg yolk
2 tablespoons Dijon mustard
25 medium shrimp, cooked
1 (15-ounce) can artichoke
  hearts, drained
2 tablespoons chopped fresh
  parsley
2 tablespoons chopped chives
1 tablespoon chopped green
  onions
Salt and pepper to taste

Combine the oil, vinegar, egg yolk and mustard in a large bowl, beating well.

Cut the shrimp and artichoke hearts into bite-size pieces. Add the shrimp, artichokes, parsley, chives, green onions, salt and pepper to the mustard mixture and stir gently to combine. Refrigerate, covered, for 2 hours.

Drain off the liquid and serve the salad on a bed of lettuce garnished with tomato wedges. Reserve the liquid for a salad dressing if desired.

Note: May substitute pasteurized egg substitute for the egg yolk.

Yield: 4 to 6 servings

Marinated Asparagus

2¹/₂ pounds asparagus
1 cup finely chopped onion
1 cup red wine vinegar
¹/₂ cup water
2 teaspoons sugar
1 teaspoon oregano
1 teaspoon tarragon
1 teaspoon dry mustard
1 teaspoon Worcestershire
  sauce
¹/₂ teaspoon salt
¹/₄ teaspoon pepper

Snap off and discard the tough stem ends of the asparagus spears. Place the asparagus in a saucepan with a small amount of boiling water. Cook for 5 minutes or until tender-crisp. Drain and rinse well under cold running water. Place in a 9 x13-inch baking dish.

Combine the onion, vinegar, water, sugar, oregano, tarragon, dry mustard, Worcestershire sauce, salt and pepper in a bowl, stirring well. Pour over the asparagus. Refrigerate, covered, for 2 to 8 hours.

Remove the asparagus from the marinade; discard the marinade. Arrange asparagus on a serving platter.

Yield: 10 servings

Fresh Broccoli Salad

2 bunches broccoli
10 slices bacon, crisp-cooked,
  crumbled
²/3 cup raisins
¹/2 cup chopped onion
1 cup mayonnaise
¹/2 cup sugar
2 tablespoons vinegar

Cut the broccoli into bite-size pieces. Combine the broccoli, bacon, raisins and onion in a bowl; mix well.

Mix the mayonnaise, sugar and vinegar in a bowl until well blended. Pour over the broccoli mixture and toss to mix. Refrigerate, covered, for 2 to 10 hours.

Yield: 12 servings

Napa Cabbage Salad

1 head napa cabbage, chopped
6 green onions with tops, sliced
2 packages ramen noodles
1 cup sliced almonds
¹/2 cup sesame seeds
¹/2 cup butter
1 cup vegetable oil
¹/2 cup vinegar
¹/2 cup sugar
3 tablespoons soy sauce
Minced garlic to taste

Combine the cabbage and green onions in a bowl; mix well and set aside.

Sauté the noodles, almonds and sesame seeds in the butter in a skillet until golden brown. Remove from the heat; cool. Add to the cabbage mixture.

Combine the oil, vinegar, sugar, soy sauce and garlic in a bowl, mixing well. Add to the cabbage mixture and toss to combine. Serve immediately.

Yield: 12 servings

Crunchy Coleslaw

1 (3-ounce) package chicken-flavor ramen noodles
1 (2-ounce) package sliced almonds
1 or 2 (1-ounce) jars sesame seeds
1 (16-ounce) package coleslaw mix
1 bunch green onions, sliced (optional)
1/2 cup vegetable oil
3 tablespoons wine vinegar
1/4 cup sugar

Break the noodles into pieces, reserving the seasoning packet. Place the noodles on a baking sheet with the almonds and sesame seeds, tossing to combine. Bake at 300 degrees for 20 minutes or until golden brown; cool.

Combine the coleslaw mix, green onions and noodle mixture in a bowl; mix well.

Mix the oil, vinegar, sugar and reserved seasoning packet in a bowl. Add to the coleslaw mixture, tossing to coat.

Yield: 8 servings

Chipparelli's Famous Baltimore Salad

1 head iceberg lettuce, chopped
2 hard-cooked eggs, chopped
1/2 cup chopped onion
1/2 cup grated Parmesan cheese
1/2 cup grated Romano cheese
1/2 cup olive oil
1/2 cup red wine vinegar
1 garlic clove, minced
1/2 teaspoon sugar or sugar substitute
1 teaspoon basil
1/2 teaspoon oregano

Combine the lettuce and eggs in a bowl; mix well and set aside.

Mix the onion, Parmesan cheese, Romano cheese, oil, vinegar, garlic, sugar, basil and oregano in a bowl, blending well. Pour over the lettuce and eggs and toss to mix. Serve immediately.

Yield: 8 servings

German Potato Salad

8 potatoes
2 hard-cooked eggs, chopped
1 rib celery, diced
1 onion, minced
4 slices bacon, diced
2 eggs, beaten
1 cup sugar
1/2 cup vinegar
1/2 cup cold water
1/2 teaspoon salt
1/4 teaspoon dry mustard
1/4 teaspoon pepper

Cook the potatoes in boiling water to cover in a saucepan until tender; drain. Cool slightly; peel and dice.

Combine the potatoes, hard-cooked eggs, celery and onion in a bowl; mix gently and set aside.

Cook the bacon in a skillet until crisp. Remove and drain on paper towels, reserving the drippings in the skillet.

Combine the beaten eggs, sugar, vinegar, water, salt, dry mustard and pepper in a bowl, mixing well. Pour into the warm (not hot) bacon drippings. Simmer over low heat for 10 minutes, stirring constantly. Pour over the potato mixture and mix well. Serve warm or cold.

Yield: 6 to 8 servings

Vegetable Medley Salad

2 (10-ounce) packages frozen peas
2 (9-ounce) packages frozen cut green beans
2 (10-ounce) packages frozen lima beans
2 cups mayonnaise
6 hard-cooked eggs, chopped
1 medium onion, finely chopped
$1/4$ cup vegetable oil
$1/4$ cup olive oil
2 teaspoons prepared yellow mustard
$1/8$ teaspoon Worcestershire sauce
$1/8$ teaspoon Tabasco sauce
4 slices bacon, crisp-cooked, crumbled

Cook the peas, green beans and lima beans according to the package directions; drain well. Place in a large bowl and cool completely.

Combine the mayonnaise, eggs, onion, vegetable oil, olive oil, mustard, Worcestershire sauce and Tabasco sauce in a bowl, blending well. Add to the vegetable mixture and stir to blend. Top with the bacon. Refrigerate, covered, until chilled.

Yield: 18 servings

Bacon Spinach Salad

2 (10-ounce) packages fresh
   spinach, torn
8 hard-cooked eggs, sliced
1 pound bacon, crisp-cooked,
   crumbled
8 ounces mushrooms, sliced
2 large heads romaine lettuce,
   torn
3/4 cup chopped red onion
16 ounces sour cream
2 cups mayonnaise
1/2 cup lemon juice
1 teaspoon salt
1/4 teaspoon pepper
1/2 cup shredded Cheddar
   cheese
1 (10-ounce) package frozen
   peas, thawed, drained

Layer the spinach, eggs, bacon, mushrooms, lettuce and onion in two 5-quart bowls.

Combine the sour cream, mayonnaise, lemon juice, salt and pepper in a bowl; mix well. Spread half evenly over the top of each salad, sealing to edge. Sprinkle with the cheese. Refrigerate, covered, for 12 to 24 hours.

Add half the peas to each salad and toss gently just before serving.

Note: Recipe may be halved or quartered. Layer the salad in clear bowls for an attractive presentation.

Yield: 50 servings

Accompaniments

Accompaniments

Artichoke and Tomato Casserole

1/2 cup chopped onion
1/4 cup butter
1 1/2 ounces cream cheese, softened
1 (15-ounce) can artichoke hearts, drained
1 (14-ounce) can diced tomatoes
1/2 cup grated Parmesan cheese

Sauté the onion in the butter in a skillet until tender. Add the cream cheese and stir until melted.

Cut the artichoke hearts into halves. Partially drain the tomatoes. Add the artichokes, tomatoes and Parmesan cheese to the cream cheese mixture and toss to combine. Spoon into a 1-quart baking dish.

Bake at 350 degrees for 40 minutes. Sprinkle with additional Parmesan cheese before serving.

Yield: 6 to 8 servings

Asparagus Carrot Squash Toss

8 ounces asparagus, cut diagonally into 1-inch pieces
8 ounces carrots, cut into julienne strips
1 yellow squash, sliced
3 tablespoons melted butter or margarine
3 tablespoons lemon juice
1 tablespoon chopped fresh dill, or 1 teaspoon dillweed
1/4 teaspoon salt

Place the asparagus, carrots and yellow squash in a steamer basket. Set over boiling water in a Dutch oven. Steam for 8 to 10 minutes or just until tender-crisp. Transfer the vegetables to a serving dish.

Combine the butter, lemon juice, dill and salt in a bowl. Pour over the vegetables and toss gently. Serve immediately.

Yield: 4 to 6 servings

Try

good ✓ thin
sautéed pork chops
perhaps!

Country Cabbage

1/4 cup chopped onion
2 tablespoons margarine
2 tablespoons flour
3/4 cup milk
1 cup shredded sharp Cheddar cheese
3/4 cup grated Parmesan cheese
5 cups diced cabbage
1 (3-ounce) can French-fried onions

Sauté the chopped onion in the margarine in a saucepan until tender. Blend in the flour. Add the milk gradually, stirring constantly. Cook until thickened, stirring constantly. Add the Cheddar cheese and 1/2 cup of the Parmesan cheese and stir until the cheeses are melted.

Place the cabbage in a 2-quart baking dish. Top with the sauce.

Bake, covered, at 350 degrees for 30 minutes. Top with the French-fried onions and remaining 1/4 cup Parmesan cheese. Bake, uncovered, for 15 minutes.

Yield: 6 to 8 servings

Carrot Casserole

1 1/2 pounds carrots, thinly sliced (4 1/2 cups)
1/2 cup mayonnaise or mayonnaise-type salad dressing
2 tablespoons chopped onion
2 tablespoons horseradish
1/4 teaspoon salt
1/8 teaspoon pepper
8 saltine crackers, crushed (1/4 cup)
2 teaspoons melted margarine

Cook the carrots in water to cover in a saucepan until tender; drain. Place in a 1-quart baking dish.

Combine the mayonnaise, onion, horseradish, salt and pepper in a bowl. Spoon over the carrots.

Mix the crackers and margarine in a bowl. Sprinkle over the top.

Bake, uncovered, at 350 degrees for 30 minutes or until heated through.

Yield: 4 to 6 servings

Country Creamed Corn

1/4 cup butter or margarine
2 1/2 cups fresh corn kernels
(8 ears)
1/2 cup milk
1 tablespoon cornstarch
1 tablespoon sugar
1/2 teaspoon salt

Melt the butter in a large skillet over medium heat. Stir in the corn and milk. Sprinkle with the cornstarch, sugar and salt and mix well.

Bring to a boil, stirring constantly. Cook for 10 to 12 minutes or until thickened, stirring constantly. Serve immediately.

Yield: 4 servings

Texan Corn Casserole

1 (16-ounce) can cream-style
corn
1 cup baking mix
1/2 cup milk
1 egg, beaten
2 tablespoons vegetable oil
1 (4-ounce) can chopped
green chiles
8 ounces shredded Monterey
Jack cheese

Combine the corn, baking mix, milk, egg and oil in a bowl, mixing well. Pour half the batter into a greased 9-inch square baking dish. Top with half the chiles and half the cheese. Top with the remaining batter, chiles and cheese.

Bake at 400 degrees for 30 to 35 minutes or until set in the center.

Yield: 6 servings

Sweet-and-Sour Green Beans

4 slices bacon
1 large onion, finely chopped
$^1/_2$ cup packed brown sugar
$^1/_4$ cup vinegar
1 teaspoon dry mustard
1 teaspoon salt
$^1/_2$ teaspoon pepper
2 (14-ounce) cans green beans

Cook the bacon in a skillet until crisp. Remove to paper towels to drain, reserving the drippings in the skillet. Crumble the bacon.

Sauté the onion in the bacon drippings until tender. Stir in the brown sugar, vinegar, dry mustard, salt and pepper. Cook, covered, over low heat for 15 to 20 minutes.

Add the undrained green beans and bacon to the skillet. Simmer, uncovered, for at least 2 hours.

Yield: 8 servings

Baby Bean Casserole

$^1/_4$ cup margarine
2 tablespoons flour
1 tablespoon chicken bouillon
  granules
1 cup water
1 (2-ounce) jar mushrooms
$^1/_4$ cup chopped onion
$^1/_4$ cup sliced green olives
2 teaspoons parsley flakes
1 (10-ounce) package frozen
  baby lima beans

Melt the margarine in a medium saucepan. Stir in the flour. Add the bouillon granules and water, stirring constantly. Cook until thickened, stirring frequently. Add the undrained mushrooms, onion, olives and parsley flakes. Remove from the heat.

Cook the lima beans according to the package directions; drain. Add to the sauce mixture. Spoon into a 2-quart baking dish.

Bake at 350 degrees for 1 hour.

Yield: 6 servings

A Helping of Tenderness

Improving the lives of those less fortunate has always been the focus of Junior League projects. One of the most notable projects that is still prospering in Parkersburg today is the Sheltered Workshop, a facility that provides paid employment opportunities to mentally and physically handicapped individuals.

The Junior League started this project in 1962 with a needs assessment and start-up funding of $5,000. Over the years the League has provided sizable financial contributions as well as volunteers to assist with fund-raising activities, developing a volunteer manual and assembling an audio-visual marketing presentation explaining the purpose of the workshop.

Since opening its doors in 1964, it has grown from a work force of 3 to serving 169 disabled individuals. It has undergone two building expansions, a name change to SW Resources, and has branched out into four divisions with many off-site work opportunities. It pays out over $800,000 a year in wages to the individuals that it serves.

Camping Beans

1 pound hot Italian sausage or bulk hot pork sausage
1 (1-ounce) envelope taco seasoning mix
2 or 3 (16-ounce) cans hot chili beans
2 teaspoons (heaping) chili powder, or to taste
1 teaspoon onion powder, or to taste
1 teaspoon garlic powder, or to taste
1^1/$_2$ slices American cheese (optional)

Remove the sausage from the casings. Brown the sausage in a Dutch oven or large cast-iron skillet, stirring until crumbly. Stir in the taco seasoning mix. Add the beans and mix well. Stir in the chili powder, onion powder and garlic powder. Cut the cheese into quarters. Place over the bean mixture.

Cook, covered, over low to medium heat for 20 to 30 minutes.

Yield: 6 to 8 servings

Eggplant Parmesan

3 eggs, beaten
Bread crumbs
1 large eggplant, peeled, sliced
3/4 cup olive oil
8 ounces shredded mozzarella
   cheese
1/2 cup grated Parmesan cheese
2 teaspoons oregano
3 (8-ounce) cans tomato sauce

Place the eggs and bread crumbs in separate shallow dishes. Dip each eggplant slice in the eggs, then in the bread crumbs to coat.

Sauté the eggplant in the oil in a skillet until golden brown on both sides.

Reserve a small amount of the mozzarella cheese for topping. Alternate layers of the eggplant, Parmesan cheese, oregano, remaining mozzarella cheese and tomato sauce in an 8-inch square baking dish until all ingredients are used, ending with tomato sauce. Top with the reserved mozzarella cheese.

Bake at 350 degrees for 30 minutes.

Yield: 6 to 8 servings

Marinated Mushrooms, Peppers and Onions

1/2 cup vegetable oil
1/4 cup soy sauce
1/4 cup dry white wine
1/4 cup corn syrup
2 teaspoons lemon juice
1/4 teaspoon ginger
3 green bell peppers, sliced
1 to 2 onions, sliced
8 ounces fresh whole
   mushrooms

Whisk the oil, soy sauce, wine, corn syrup, lemon juice and ginger in a bowl until well mixed. Add the green peppers, onions and mushrooms. Refrigerate, covered, for at least 5 hours, stirring occasionally.

Place the vegetables on a piece of foil. Grill for about 20 minutes or until tender, shaking the foil occasionally.

Note: Recipe may be doubled.

Yield: 4 servings

Try

Herb Potato Casserole

8 to 10 white potatoes
$1/2$ cup light cream
$1/4$ cup butter or margarine
2 eggs, beaten
1 (4-ounce) can pimentos,
　drained, diced
1 teaspoon onion powder
$1/2$ teaspoon oregano
$1/2$ teaspoon basil
$1/2$ teaspoon marjoram
$1/4$ teaspoon baking powder
Salt and pepper to taste
1 cup shredded sharp Cheddar
　cheese

Cook the potatoes in boiling water until tender; drain. Cool slightly; peel.

Place the potatoes in a bowl and mash well. Stir in the cream, butter, eggs, pimentos, onion powder, oregano, basil, marjoram, baking powder, salt and pepper. Spoon into a greased 2-quart baking dish. Top with the cheese.

Bake at 350 degrees for 25 to 30 minutes or until heated through.

Note: May be made a day in advance and refrigerated. Increase the baking time to 30 to 35 minutes.

Yield: 8 to 10 servings

116

Try

Picnic Potato Cheese Casserole

2 pounds frozen hash brown
    potatoes
1 onion, chopped
1 (10-ounce) can cream of
    chicken soup
16 ounces sour cream
8 ounces shredded Cheddar
    cheese
1 cup crushed potato chips
1/2 cup margarine,
    cut into pieces

Thaw the potatoes at room temperature for 30 minutes. Combine the potatoes, onion, soup, sour cream and cheese in a bowl. Spoon into a buttered 9x13-inch baking dish. Top with the potato chips. Dot with the margarine.

Bake at 375 degrees for 1 hour.

Yield: 12 servings

Second-Helpings Sweet Potato Casserole

1 (40-ounce) can sweet
    potatoes, drained
3/4 cup sugar
1/2 cup milk
1/4 cup butter, softened
2 eggs, beaten
1/4 teaspoon cinnamon
1/4 teaspoon ground cloves
1 cup crushed cornflakes
1/2 cup packed brown sugar
1/2 cup melted butter
1/2 cup shredded coconut
1/2 cup chopped pecans or
    walnuts

Mash the sweet potatoes in a bowl until smooth. Blend in the sugar, milk, 1/4 cup butter, eggs, cinnamon and cloves. Spoon into a buttered 2-quart baking dish.

Bake at 400 degrees for 20 minutes.

Combine the cornflakes, brown sugar, melted butter, coconut and pecans in a bowl. Spread evenly over the top of the sweet potatoes. Bake for 15 minutes.

Yield: 8 servings

Jalapeño Spinach

1 medium onion, chopped
$^1/_2$ cup butter
8 ounces cream cheese,
    cut into cubes
2 (10-ounce) packages frozen
    chopped spinach
1 teaspoon chopped jalapeño
    pepper
1 cup fresh bread crumbs
$^1/_4$ cup melted butter

Sauté the onion in the $^1/_2$ cup butter in a large skillet until tender. Add the cream cheese, stirring until melted. Remove from the heat.

Cook the spinach according to the package directions; drain. Add the spinach and jalapeño pepper to the onion mixture, blending well.

Spoon the spinach mixture into a greased 1-quart baking dish. Combine the bread crumbs and the $^1/_4$ cup melted butter in a bowl. Sprinkle over the top.

Bake at 350 degrees for 30 minutes or until heated through.

Note: Recipe may be doubled. May substitute 20 ounces fresh spinach leaves for the frozen spinach.

Yield: 4 to 6 servings

Summer Squash Casserole

2 cups diced yellow squash
$^1/_2$ cup diced onion
$^1/_2$ teaspoon salt
1 (10-ounce) can cream of
    chicken soup
$^1/_2$ cup sour cream
1 carrot, shredded
$^1/_2$ teaspoon seasoned salt
1 cup dried bread crumbs
$^1/_4$ cup melted butter

Parboil the squash and onion in salted water in a saucepan; drain. Stir in the soup, sour cream, carrot and seasoned salt. Spoon into a 1-quart baking dish.

Combine the bread crumbs and butter in a bowl. Sprinkle over the squash mixture.

Bake at 350 degrees for 30 minutes or until bubbly.

Yield: 6 to 8 servings

Veggie-Stuffed Tomatoes

6 large ripe tomatoes
$1/2$ cup finely chopped onion
$1/2$ cup finely chopped green
   bell pepper
2 tablespoons margarine
3 cups cooked white rice
1 cup corn kernels
$1/2$ teaspoon salt
$1/4$ teaspoon pepper
$1 1/4$ cups shredded provolone
   or mozzarella cheese
$1/2$ cup sliced black olives
Paprika

Cut a slice from the top of each tomato; discard slices. Scoop out the tomato pulp and reserve. Set the tomato shells aside.

Sauté the onion and green pepper in the margarine in a large skillet until tender. Stir in the rice, corn, tomato pulp, salt and pepper. Simmer for about 5 minutes. Stir in 1 cup of the cheese and olives. Remove from the heat.

Spoon the rice mixture into the tomato shells. Place the stuffed tomatoes in a 9x13-inch baking dish. Pour in enough water to reach a $1/4$-inch depth. Sprinkle the remaining $1/4$ cup cheese and paprika over the tops of the tomatoes. Spoon any remaining rice mixture into a separate baking dish and bake alongside the stuffed tomatoes.

Bake at 375 degrees for 20 to 25 minutes or until heated through.

Yield: 6 servings

Try

New Orleans Tomatoes

1 large green bell pepper,
   chopped
1 large onion, chopped
3 tablespoons butter
6 to 7 medium tomatoes,
   cut into quarters
1 tablespoon chopped fresh
   thyme
$1/8$ teaspoon cayenne pepper
Salt to taste
2 tablespoons finely chopped
   fresh parsley

Sauté the green pepper and onion in the butter in a large skillet over medium heat for 10 minutes or until the onion is lightly browned.

Stir in the tomatoes, thyme and cayenne. Cook for 5 to 6 minutes, stirring often. Season with salt and sprinkle with the parsley. Serve immediately.

Yield: 6 servings

Try

Garden Vegetables with Horseradish Sauce

3 cups cauliflower florets
2 carrots, sliced $1/2$ inch thick
1 pound broccoli, cut into
   1-inch pieces
1 cup mayonnaise
$1/4$ cup finely chopped onion
3 tablespoons horseradish
$1/4$ teaspoon salt
$1/8$ teaspoon pepper
$1/2$ cup fine dry bread crumbs
2 tablespoons melted butter
$1/8$ teaspoon paprika

Cook the cauliflower and carrots in a small amount of boiling water in a 3-quart saucepan for 5 minutes. Add the broccoli. Cook for 5 minutes or until the vegetables are tender-crisp; drain. Place in a large bowl.

Combine the mayonnaise, onion, horseradish, salt and pepper in a small bowl. Pour over the vegetables and toss to mix. Spoon into a buttered 2-quart baking dish.

Combine the bread crumbs, butter and paprika in a small bowl. Sprinkle over the vegetables.

Bake, uncovered, at 350 degrees for 15 minutes or until heated through and topping is golden brown.

Yield: 8 to 10 servings

Shrimp Lo Mein Noodles

2 tablespoons vegetable oil

1/2 teaspoon sesame oil

1 pound shrimp, peeled, deveined

1 package lo mein noodles, cooked

1 garlic clove, minced

1/4 medium head cabbage, sliced

1/2 medium carrot, sliced

1/4 cup oyster sauce

1 tablespoon soy paste

Heat the vegetable and sesame oils in a wok or large skillet until hot. Add the shrimp. Stir-fry just until the shrimp turn pink. Add the noodles and garlic. Stir-fry until heated through. Add the cabbage, carrot, oyster sauce and soy paste. Stir-fry for 3 minutes.

Note: May substitute 1 pound sliced chicken, beef or pork for the shrimp. Soy paste is available at Asian markets.

Yield: 4 servings

Add a Dash of Folk Music

The Junior League of Parkersburg has always taken an interest in promoting the arts to children. In 1968 the members began exploring and researching the idea of publishing a songbook for children. Their research led them to Dr. Marie Boette, a local music scholar.

Dr. Boette, together with the Junior League, believed that preserving the musical heritage of West Virginia was an important and worthwhile endeavor. From this partnership, Singa Hipsy Doodle and Other Folk Songs of West Virginia was born, with Dr. Boette serving as the editor of the book.

The collection of folk songs was published in 1972, and copies of the book were provided to local schools and libraries.

Maybe

Company Rice

1 cup uncooked white rice
1 cup chopped onion
1/2 cup melted butter
2 (10-ounce) cans beef
    consommé
1/2 cup seedless raisins
1/2 cup chopped peanuts
1/2 cup chopped celery
1 (4-ounce) can sliced
    mushrooms, drained

Sauté the rice and onion in the butter in a skillet until browned.

Add the consommé, raisins, peanuts, celery and mushrooms and mix well. Spoon into a 1 1/2-quart baking dish.

Bake, uncovered, at 300 degrees for about 1 hour or until the rice is tender.

Yield: 8 servings

A Large Portion of Thriftiness

The Junior League Thrift Shop was opened in 1932 to establish a regular means of revenue to support League projects, with the initial year of operation raising $200. League members donated gently used items and worked daily shifts to staff the shop. It became the main source of funding for the organization for many years, except during the World War II period when the shop had to close temporarily because the women were needed elsewhere in the community.

In 1988, the shop was turned over to the Association for Retarded Citizens, the ARC, and the name was changed to Noah's Arc. The store continues to operate today and has expanded to two locations.

Now, the "Whale-of-a-Sale" fills the void of the Thrift Shop. League members donate their used items and work at the giant, 1-day yard sale. The "Whale" is the League's largest annual fund-raiser.

Brown Rice with Nuts and Raisins

1/2 cup golden raisins

1/2 cup dry white wine

1/4 cup chopped onion

1/4 cup butter

1 cup uncooked brown rice

2 1/2 cups chicken stock
   or water

1/2 teaspoon salt

1/4 teaspoon pepper

2 tablespoons melted unsalted
   butter

3/4 cup toasted slivered
   almonds

1/2 cup chopped fresh mint
   or cilantro

Combine the raisins and wine in a bowl. Let stand at room temperature until the raisins are plumped; set aside.

Sauté the onion in 1/4 cup butter in a skillet until tender. Add the rice. Cook over low heat for 3 minutes or until the rice is lightly browned and coated with butter.

Add the stock, salt and pepper, stirring to mix. Bring to a boil. Simmer, covered, over low heat for 45 minutes or until the liquid is absorbed. Remove from the heat.

Add the melted butter and toss to mix. Stir in the almonds, raisins and mint. Spoon into a serving bowl and garnish with additional mint.

Yield: 4 servings

Cranberry Apple Chutney

2 cups fresh or frozen cranberries
1/2 cup water
1/4 cup packed brown sugar
1 Bosc pear, chopped
1/2 Granny Smith apple, chopped
1/2 cup chopped celery
3 tablespoons golden raisins
2 tablespoons toasted chopped
   walnuts
2 tablespoons apple
   cider vinegar
1 1/2 teaspoons grated gingerroot
1 teaspoon cinnamon
1 1/2 teaspoons grated
   orange zest

Place the cranberries, water and brown sugar in a saucepan. Bring to a boil, stirring often. Cook for 5 minutes or until the cranberries pop.

Stir in the pear, apple, celery, raisins, walnuts, vinegar, gingerroot and cinnamon. Simmer over low heat for 20 minutes.

Stir in the orange zest. Refrigerate, covered, until chilled.

Note: To toast walnuts, place on a baking sheet and bake at 350 degrees for 10 minutes.

Yield: 10 to 12 servings

Desserts

Desserts

Glazed Apple Cake

4 cups sliced peeled apples
2 cups sugar
2 cups flour
1 cup (scant) vegetable oil
2 eggs, beaten
2 teaspoons vanilla extract
2 teaspoons cinnamon
1 1/2 teaspoons baking soda
1 teaspoon salt
1/2 cup margarine
3/4 cup sugar
1/2 cup milk

Combine the apples, 2 cups sugar, flour, oil, eggs, vanilla, cinnamon, baking soda and salt in a bowl, stirring just until well mixed. Spoon into a greased 9x13-inch baking pan.

Bake at 350 degrees for 45 minutes.

Combine the margarine, 3/4 cup sugar and milk in a saucepan. Bring to a boil; boil for 2 minutes, stirring constantly. Pour over the hot cake. Cool completely.

Yield: 15 servings

Blueberry Pudding Cake

2 cups fresh or frozen
 blueberries
1 teaspoon cinnamon
1 teaspoon lemon juice
1 cup flour
$1^{1}/_{2}$ cups sugar
1 teaspoon baking powder
$^{1}/_{2}$ cup milk
3 tablespoons melted butter or
 margarine
1 tablespoon cornstarch
1 cup boiling water

Toss the blueberries, cinnamon and lemon juice in a bowl. Spoon into a greased 8- or 9-inch square baking dish.

Combine the flour, $^{3}/_{4}$ cup of the sugar and baking powder in a bowl. Stir in the milk and butter. Spoon over the blueberries.

Combine the remaining $^{3}/_{4}$ cup sugar and cornstarch in a bowl. Sprinkle over the batter. Pour the boiling water slowly over the top.

Bake at 350 degrees for 45 to 50 minutes or until a wooden pick inserted in the center comes out clean. Serve with ice cream if desired.

Yield: 9 servings

To-Kill-For Carrot Cake

2 cups flour
1 tablespoon baking powder
2 teaspoons cinnamon
1/2 teaspoon baking soda
1/2 teaspoon salt
1 cup sugar
3 eggs
1 cup applesauce
1/2 cup vegetable oil
4 cups finely chopped carrots
2 cups confectioners' sugar
8 ounces light cream cheese,
   softened

Combine the flour, baking powder, cinnamon, baking soda and salt in a bowl; set aside.

Beat the sugar and eggs in a large bowl. Stir in the applesauce and oil. Blend in the flour mixture. Stir in the carrots. Spoon into a 9x13-inch baking pan sprayed with nonstick cooking spray.

Bake at 350 degrees for 35 to 40 minutes or until a wooden pick inserted in the center comes out clean. Cool completely on a wire rack.

Beat the confectioners' sugar and cream cheese in a bowl until smooth. Spread over the top of the cake. Sprinkle with chopped nuts if desired.

Note: Use a food processor to easily chop the carrots.

Yield: 12 servings

Hot Fudge Sundae Cake

1 1/2 cups flour
1 cup plus 2 tablespoons sugar
3 tablespoons baking cocoa
1 tablespoon baking powder
1/2 teaspoon salt
3/4 cup milk
3 tablespoons vegetable oil
1 1/2 teaspoons vanilla extract
1 1/2 cups packed brown sugar
6 tablespoons baking cocoa
1 3/4 cups hot water

Combine the flour, sugar, 3 tablespoons baking cocoa, baking powder and salt in an ungreased 9x13-inch baking pan and mix well.

Combine the milk, oil and vanilla in a bowl. Stir the milk mixture into the dry ingredients in the pan with a fork. Spread the batter evenly in the pan.

Mix the brown sugar and 6 tablespoons baking cocoa in a bowl. Sprinkle evenly over the batter. Do not stir. Pour the hot water over the top.

Bake at 350 degrees for 40 minutes. Let stand for 15 minutes. Serve with vanilla ice cream.

Yield: 15 servings

Chocolate Turtle Cake

1 (2-layer) package German
   chocolate cake mix
1 (14-ounce) can sweetened
   condensed milk
$1/2$ cup melted butter
1 (14-ounce) package caramels
1 cup butter
$1^1/2$ cups chocolate chips
1 cup pecan pieces
$1/4$ cup baking cocoa
5 teaspoons evaporated milk
Confectioners' sugar

Prepare the cake mix using package directions. Pour half the batter into a bowl. Stir in $1/2$ can of condensed milk and $1/2$ cup melted butter. Pour into a greased 9x13-inch pan. Bake at 350 degrees for 25 minutes.

Place the caramels, half of the 1 cup butter and remaining $1/2$ can condensed milk in a saucepan. Heat over low heat until the butter and caramels are melted, stirring frequently. Pour the caramel mixture over the hot cake. Sprinkle with the chocolate chips and pecans. Pour the remaining cake batter over the top. Bake for 30 minutes. Cool in the pan on a wire rack.

Melt the remaining $1/2$ cup butter with the baking cocoa and evaporated milk in a saucepan. Bring to a boil; reduce the heat to low. Stir in enough confectioners' sugar to reach desired icing consistency. Spread over the top of the cake. Cut into small squares to serve.

Yield: 24 servings

A Dash of Tenderness

Because of the Junior League Well Baby Clinic, thousands of children under the age of six received complete physical examinations by doctors and nurses from the County Health Department with Junior League committee members providing assistance. Comprehensive medical records were kept in each case, and follow-up visits for the more needy families were completed.

Eyeglasses, full immunizations, cod liver oil, and prescriptions were provided. If surgical interventions such as tonsillectomies were necessary, arrangements were made. Follow-up visits continued until defects were corrected.

The Clinic was closed due to a shortage of doctors as a result of World War II. The Junior League Well Baby Clinic was turned over to the Wood County Health Department in 1943.

Grandma's Fig Preserve Cake

1 cup buttermilk
1 cup vegetable oil
3 eggs
1¹/₂ cups sugar
2 cups sifted flour
1 teaspoon baking soda
1 teaspoon salt
¹/₂ teaspoon cinnamon
¹/₂ teaspoon allspice
1 cup chopped pecans or
   walnuts
1 cup fig preserves
1 teaspoon vanilla extract
1 cup sugar
¹/₂ cup buttermilk
6 tablespoons butter, softened
¹/₂ teaspoon baking soda

Blend the 1 cup buttermilk, oil and eggs in a bowl. Beat in the 1¹/₂ cups sugar. Add the flour, 1 teaspoon baking soda, salt, cinnamon and allspice and mix well. Stir in the pecans, preserves and vanilla. Pour into a greased and floured 10-inch tube or bundt pan.

Bake at 325 degrees for 55 minutes. Cool in the pan for 10 minutes. Remove from the pan and cool slightly on a wire rack.

Combine the 1 cup sugar, ¹/₂ cup buttermilk, butter and ¹/₂ teaspoon baking soda in a saucepan. Cook to 234 to 240 degrees on a candy thermometer, soft-ball stage, stirring constantly. Spread over the warm cake.

Yield: 16 servings

Italian Cream Cake

1 cup margarine or butter,
  softened
2 cups sugar
5 egg yolks
2 cups sifted flour
1 teaspoon baking soda
1 cup buttermilk
1 cup chopped pecans
1 (7-ounce) can shredded
  coconut
1 teaspoon vanilla extract
5 egg whites
Cream Cheese Frosting
1/2 cup chopped walnuts

Cream the margarine and sugar in a mixer bowl until light and fluffy. Add the egg yolks 1 at a time, beating well after each addition.

Sift the flour and baking soda together. Add to the egg mixture alternately with the buttermilk, mixing well after each addition. Stir in the pecans, coconut and vanilla.

Beat the egg whites in a mixer bowl until soft peaks form. Fold into the cake batter. Pour into 3 greased 9-inch cake pans.

Bake at 350 degrees for 40 minutes. Cool in the pans for 10 minutes. Remove from the pans and cool completely on wire racks. Spread the frosting between the layers and over the top of the cake. Sprinkle the walnuts over the top.

Cream Cheese Frosting

8 ounces cream cheese,
  softened
1/2 cup margarine or butter,
  softened
1 (1-pound) package
  confectioners' sugar
1 teaspoon vanilla extract

Beat the cream cheese and margarine in a mixer bowl until light and fluffy. Add the confectioners' sugar and vanilla, beating until smooth. If the frosting is too stiff to spread, beat in a small amount of milk.

Yield: 12 servings

Mandarin Orange Cake

1 (2-layer) package yellow
   pudding recipe cake mix
4 eggs
3/4 cup vegetable oil
1 (11-ounce) can mandarin
   oranges
1 (15-ounce) can unsweetened
   juice-pack crushed pineapple
1 (4-ounce) package vanilla
   instant pudding mix
8 ounces whipped topping

Blend the cake mix, eggs, oil and undrained oranges in a bowl until well mixed. Pour into a greased and floured 9x13-inch baking pan.

Bake at 325 degrees for 40 minutes. Cool completely on a wire rack.

Drain 1/4 cup juice from the pineapple. Combine the remaining pineapple juice, pineapple and pudding mix in a bowl. Fold in the whipped topping. Spread over the top of the cake. Refrigerate until ready to serve. Store any leftovers in the refrigerator.

Yield: 16 servings

A Healthy Serving of Service

The Junior League mission statement from the early twenties and even today touches on "service" and "volunteerism." Throughout the rich history of the Junior League of Parkersburg, our members have dedicated hours to many community efforts.

These efforts include recruiting blood donors for the Red Cross; chaperoning youth dances at the YWCA; working at children's wards in local hospitals; selling pins to increase awareness of tuberculosis; ringing Salvation Army bells at local shopping centers during the holiday season; working at the Wood County Crippled Children's Treatment Center; assisting the staff of the Kaleidoscope, an interactive art mobile for children; and manning a well-baby display at the local 4-H Fair. The list could go on and on.

As with all Leagues, these types of volunteer hours don't include the many hours our members invest in community boards and organizations where they provide leadership and direction to further enhance the community we live in.

Try

Peach Almond Pound Cake

1 cup butter, softened
3 cups sugar
6 eggs
3 cups flour
$1/2$ teaspoon salt
$1/4$ teaspoon baking soda
1 cup mashed peaches
$1/2$ cup sour cream
1 teaspoon vanilla extract
1 teaspoon almond extract

Beat the butter in a mixer bowl. Add the sugar gradually, beating at medium speed until light and fluffy. Add the eggs 1 at a time, beating well after each addition.

Combine the flour, salt and baking soda in a bowl. Combine the peaches and sour cream in a bowl. Add the flour mixture to the butter mixture alternately with the peach mixture, beginning and ending with the flour mixture. Mix just until blended after each addition. Stir in the vanilla and almond extracts. Pour the batter into 2 greased and floured 5x9-inch loaf pans.

Bake at 350 degrees for 1 hour and 5 minutes or until a wooden pick inserted in the centers comes out clean. Cool in the pans for 10 to 15 minutes. Remove from the pans and cool completely on wire racks.

Yield: 24 servings

135

Peanut Butter Cake

1 cup water
1/2 cup margarine
1/2 cup vegetable oil
1/3 cup peanut butter
2 cups flour
2 cups sugar
1/2 cup milk
2 eggs, slightly beaten
1 teaspoon baking soda
1 teaspoon vanilla extract
1/2 cup margarine
1/2 cup peanut butter
1/2 cup milk
1 teaspoon vanilla extract
1 to 1 1/2 (1-pound) packages
   confectioners' sugar

Place the water, 1/2 cup margarine, oil and 1/3 cup peanut butter in a large saucepan. Bring to a boil, stirring constantly. Remove from the heat; set aside.

Combine the flour, sugar, 1/2 cup milk, eggs, baking soda and 1 teaspoon vanilla in a bowl. Add to the boiled mixture and mix well. Pour into a greased and floured 9x13-inch baking pan.

Bake at 350 degrees for 40 minutes. Cool on a wire rack.

Combine 1/2 cup margarine, 1/2 cup peanut butter and 1/2 cup milk in a saucepan. Bring to a boil, stirring constantly. Remove from the heat. Beat in 1 teaspoon vanilla and enough confectioners' sugar to reach desired frosting consistency. Spread over the top of the cake.

Note: May also bake the cake in a greased and floured 10x15-inch baking pan. Reduce the baking time to 20 to 25 minutes.

Yield: 15 servings

Try

Cream Cheese Pound Cake

1 cup margarine, softened
1/2 cup butter, softened
8 ounces cream cheese,
  softened
3 cups sugar
6 eggs
3 cups flour
1 teaspoon vanilla extract

Beat the margarine, butter and cream cheese in a mixer bowl. Add the sugar and beat until light and fluffy. Add the eggs alternately with the flour, ending with the flour and beating well after each addition. Beat in the vanilla. Pour into a greased and floured 10-inch tube pan.

Bake at 325 degrees for 1 hour and 25 minutes. Do not open the oven door during the baking process. Cool in the pan for 10 minutes. Remove from the pan to a wire rack to cool completely.

Yield: 16 servings

A Cup of Love

In 1972 the West Virginia Welfare Department (now the West Virginia Department of Health and Human Resources) needed information on the state foster care system. It called on the Junior League of Parkersburg for help.

League members investigated and wrote case studies on forty-seven foster homes overseen by the state. This allowed overworked and overwhelmed social workers the opportunity to concentrate on other duties while the Department got the valuable information that it needed.

To show its appreciation, the State Welfare Department designated the Junior League of Parkersburg the 1974 "Outstanding Organization of West Virginia."

The League went on to mount an extensive radio and television campaign to find foster homes for abused and neglected children in the welfare system.

Pumpkin Pie Cake

1 (29-ounce) can pumpkin
1 (12-ounce) can evaporated
milk
1 cup sugar
3 eggs
1 tablespoon cinnamon
$1/4$ to $1/2$ teaspoon salt
1 (2-layer) package yellow or
spice cake mix
1 cup chopped pecans or
walnuts
$3/4$ cup melted margarine

Combine the pumpkin, evaporated milk, sugar, eggs, cinnamon and salt in a bowl and mix well. Pour into a 9x13-inch baking pan sprayed with nonstick cooking spray. Sprinkle the cake mix and pecans over the top. Drizzle with the margarine.

Bake at 350 degrees for 50 minutes. Cool completely on a wire rack. Serve with whipped cream.

Yield: 15 servings

Try

Punch Bowl Cake

1 (6-ounce) package vanilla
pudding and pie filling mix
1 angel food cake, cut into
cubes
1 (21-ounce) can blueberry or
cherry pie filling
1 banana, sliced
1 (8-ounce) can crushed
pineapple, drained
Fresh or thawed frozen
raspberries, strawberries
and/or blueberries
Whipped topping
Shaved choc.
almonds

Prepare the pudding mix using package directions; do not chill.

Layer half the cake cubes and half the warm pudding in a trifle bowl or punch bowl. Top with the pie filling and banana. Layer the remaining cake cubes and pudding over the banana. Top with the pineapple and desired amount of berries. Spread with whipped topping to cover. Refrigerate, covered, until chilled. Garnish with shaved chocolate and almonds.

Yield: 12 servings

A Tablespoon of Community Services

In 1949, the Junior League of Parkersburg saw the need for a clinic to diagnose and treat behavior problems in children whose parents couldn't afford to pay for professional services of this type. To meet this need, the League established the community's first Child Behavior Clinic.

Trained professionals worked with patients while the Junior League provided the funding to operate the clinic and League members to serve as receptionists and clerical staff. League members also made presentations throughout the community to educate the public about the services that the clinic offered.

Services were broadened to include treatment for adults, and the program was recognized throughout the state as the only such clinic in West Virginia to be sponsored and operated locally, by the community. A full ten years after the clinic began, the West Virginia Department of Mental Health provided full funding.

Today, Westbrook Health Services, Inc., remains a private, not-for-profit agency offering services to an eight-county area in western West Virginia. It employs over 500 people and has an annual budget in excess of $18 million.

Amaretto Truffles

12 ounces semisweet chocolate,
  finely chopped
1 cup whipping cream
1 tablespoon amaretto
1/2 cup baking cocoa
3/4 cup finely chopped almonds,
  lightly toasted

Place the chocolate in a medium bowl. Bring the cream to a boil in a saucepan. Pour over the chocolate. Let stand for 1 minute. Whisk vigorously until the chocolate melts completely and the mixture is smooth. Add the amaretto and whisk until smooth. Refrigerate, loosely covered with plastic wrap, for 6 to 10 hours or until firm.

Remove the chocolate mixture from the refrigerator and let stand at room temperature for 15 minutes. Place the baking cocoa and almonds in separate shallow bowls.

Scoop out a small amount of the chocolate mixture with a melon baller or small teaspoon for each truffle. Roll the truffles into small balls with your hands; the balls should not be perfectly smooth so they resemble real truffles.

Roll half the truffles in the baking cocoa, shaking off any excess cocoa. Roll the other half in the almonds, pressing them lightly into the surface to adhere. Transfer the coated truffles to a tray.

Store in a tightly covered container in a cool, dry place for up to 1 week. Do not store in the refrigerator. If the cocoa coating absorbs into the truffles, dust with more cocoa before serving.

Note: May substitute Cognac, Grand Marnier, framboise or other flavored liqueurs for the amaretto.

Yield: 3 dozen truffles

Compliments of the Greenbrier Hotel

Try

Chocolate Peanut Clusters

1 cup butterscotch chips
1 cup chocolate chips
2 tablespoons peanut butter
2 cups salted Spanish peanuts

Place the butterscotch chips, chocolate chips and peanut butter in a 2-quart heavy saucepan. Cook over low heat until the chips are melted and the mixture is smooth, stirring constantly. Remove from the heat. Stir in the peanuts.

Drop by rounded teaspoonfuls onto baking sheets lined with waxed paper. Refrigerate until firm. Store in a covered container in the refrigerator.

Yield: 48 clusters

White Chocolate Party Mix

5 cups Cheerios
5 cups rice Chex
5 cups miniature pretzel
  twists
2 cups peanuts
1 pound "M & M's" Plain
  Chocolate Candies
2 (12-ounce) packages white
  chocolate chips
3 tablespoons vegetable oil

Combine the Cheerios, rice Chex, pretzels, peanuts and "M & M's" in a large bowl.

Melt the white chocolate chips with the oil in a saucepan over low heat, stirring constantly. Pour over the cereal mixture and stir to coat. Spread the cereal mixture on waxed paper. Let stand until cool. Store in airtight containers.

Yield: about 20 cups

try

Meringue Kisses

2 egg whites, at room
    temperature
$1/8$ teaspoon salt
$1/8$ teaspoon cream of tartar
1 teaspoon vanilla extract
$3/4$ cup sugar
1 cup semisweet
    chocolate chips

Beat the egg whites, salt and cream of tartar in a large mixer bowl until foamy. Add the sugar 2 tablespoons at a time, beating constantly until the egg whites form stiff glossy peaks. Fold in the chocolate chips.

Drop the egg white mixture by teaspoonfuls onto cookie sheets.

Bake at 300 degrees for 20 to 25 minutes or until dry.

Yield: about 3 dozen

try

Fannie May's Pralines

2 cups packed brown sugar
$2/3$ cup margarine
$1/4$ cup water
2 cups pecan halves

Place the brown sugar, margarine and water in a saucepan. Bring to a boil. Stir in the pecans. Cook to 234 to 240 degrees on a candy thermometer, soft-ball stage, stirring constantly.

Drop by teaspoonfuls onto foil. Let stand at room temperature until hardened.

Yield: 50 pralines

Peanut Brittle

3 cups sugar
1 cup light corn syrup
$^1/_2$ cup water
3 cups raw peanuts
1 tablespoon baking soda
1 tablespoon butter
1 teaspoon salt

Combine the sugar, corn syrup and water in a saucepan. Cook to 230 to 240 degrees on a candy thermometer, thread stage.

Add the peanuts. Cook to 300 to 310 degrees on a candy thermometer, hard-crack stage, stirring constantly. The mixture will turn light brown.

Remove from the heat. Add the baking soda, butter and salt and stir until well mixed. Pour onto a buttered baking sheet. Spread as thinly as possible. Let stand at room temperature until hardened.

Yield: $2^1/_2$ pounds

An Equal Measure of Equality

The Junior League of Parkersburg took action in support of a bill introduced in the 1955 session of the West Virginia Legislature to amend the State Constitution to permit women to serve on juries. Lobbying efforts on the part of League members led to the passage of the bill, and the question was placed before the voters in the 1956 general election.

The League teamed up with several other women's organizations, the League of Women Voters, the American Association of University Women, and the Business and Professional Women, and began a statewide educational campaign to secure passage of the Jury Service Amendment.

The amendment went on to pass in the general election.

Chocolate Almond Biscotti

1¹/₂ cups flour
¹/₂ cup baking cocoa
1¹/₂ teaspoons baking powder
¹/₂ teaspoon baking soda
²/₃ cup sugar
2 eggs
2 tablespoons butter, softened
¹/₂ to 1 teaspoon almond
   extract
¹/₂ cup chopped or slivered
   almonds
1 cup semisweet chocolate
   chips (optional)

Combine the flour, baking cocoa, baking powder and baking soda in a bowl; set aside.

Beat the sugar, eggs, butter and almond extract in a large bowl until creamy. Add the flour mixture gradually, beating constantly. Stir in the almonds and chocolate chips.

Divide the dough into 2 equal portions. Shape each half into a 12-inch long log. Flatten the tops of the logs slightly. Place on a greased baking sheet.

Bake at 350 degrees for 25 minutes. Cool on a wire rack for 5 minutes. Cut the logs into ¹/₂-inch-thick slices. Return to the baking sheet, cut sides down.

Bake for 20 minutes. Cool completely on wire racks.

Yield: 4 dozen

Chocolate Caramel Layer Squares

1 (14-ounce) package caramels
$^2/3$ cup evaporated milk
1 (2-layer) package German
   chocolate cake mix
6 tablespoons margarine or
   butter, softened
1 cup chopped walnuts
1 cup chocolate chips

Place the caramels and $^1/3$ cup of the evaporated milk in the top of a double boiler. Cook over simmering water until the caramels are melted, stirring constantly. Remove from the heat; set aside.

Combine the cake mix, remaining $^1/3$ cup evaporated milk, margarine and walnuts in a bowl. Stir until a dough forms. Press $^1/3$ of the dough mixture into a greased 9x13-inch baking pan.

Bake at 350 degrees for 6 minutes. Remove from the oven.

Sprinkle with the chocolate chips. Pour the caramel mixture over the chips and spread evenly. Crumble the remaining dough and sprinkle over the top.

Bake for 18 minutes. Cool completely on a wire rack. Refrigerate, covered, until chilled. Cut into squares.

Yield: 2 dozen

Super Boutique Chocos

1 cup butter, softened

1 cup corn oil margarine, softened

2 cups packed brown sugar

2 cups sugar

4 eggs

2 teaspoons vanilla extract

5 cups rolled oats

4 cups self-rising flour

2 teaspoons baking powder

2 teaspoons baking soda

1 teaspoon salt

4 cups chocolate chips

2 ounces unsweetened chocolate, grated

2 ounces German's sweet chocolate, grated

Beat the butter, margarine, brown sugar and sugar in a mixer bowl until light and fluffy. Add the eggs and vanilla and mix well.

Process the oats in a blender or food processor container until powdery. Pour into a bowl. Stir in the flour, baking powder, baking soda and salt. Add to the butter mixture and mix well. Stir in the chocolate chips, unsweetened chocolate and German's chocolate.

Form dough into 1-inch rounds. Place 2 inches apart on ungreased cookie sheets.

Bake at 375 degrees for 9 minutes. Cool completely on wire racks.

Yield: 9 dozen

Double-Chocolate Crinkles

1/2 cup shortening
4 ounces unsweetened chocolate
2 cups sugar
2 tablespoons vanilla extract
4 eggs
2 cups flour
2 teaspoons baking powder
1/2 teaspoon salt
1 cup chocolate chips
1 cup sifted confectioners' sugar

Melt the shortening and unsweetened chocolate in a saucepan. Stir in the sugar. Pour into a bowl; cool. Beat until blended.

Add the vanilla and mix well. Add the eggs 1 at a time, beating well after each addition.

Combine the flour, baking powder and salt in a bowl. Stir into the chocolate mixture. Add the chocolate chips and blend well. Refrigerate, covered, for 3 to 8 hours.

Roll the dough into 1-inch balls. Roll in the confectioners' sugar to coat. Place 2 inches apart on greased cookie sheets.

Bake for 8 to 10 minutes. Cookies will be soft. Cool completely on wire racks.

Yield: about 4 dozen

Add a Twist of Fun

For seventy-four years, the League has never faltered from an interest in social activities. From the first Cabaret and Charity Balls in 1925 to the 1998 tea honoring Provisionals and holiday luncheons for Sustainers, new opportunities for social gatherings have always had importance.

As we approach the millennium, we are faced with the challenges of finding time to relax while working outside of the home and still balancing life with church and family and daily routine. Members are always trying new ideas to have fun whether it is a new twist to the annual Spring Charity Ball or Easter Egg Hunts or Halloween parties that include our "little ones." With the League's seventy-fifth anniversary approaching, a definite "social" activity will be in the making.

Black Bottom Cookies

8 ounces cream cheese,
  softened
$1/3$ cup sugar
1 egg
$1/8$ teaspoon salt
2 cups chocolate chips
$1^{1}/_{2}$ cups flour
1 cup sugar
$1/4$ cup baking cocoa
1 teaspoon baking soda
$1/2$ teaspoon salt
1 cup water
$1/3$ cup vegetable oil
1 tablespoon white vinegar
1 teaspoon vanilla extract

Combine the cream cheese, $1/3$ cup sugar, egg and $1/8$ teaspoon salt in a bowl, mixing well. Stir in the chocolate chips; set aside.

Combine the flour, 1 cup sugar, baking cocoa, baking soda and $1/2$ teaspoon salt in a bowl. Add the water, oil, vinegar and vanilla and mix well.

Fill paper-lined miniature muffin cups $1/3$ full with the chocolate mixture. Top each with $1/2$ to $3/4$ teaspoon of the cream cheese mixture.

Bake at 350 degrees for 15 to 18 minutes. Do not overbake.

Yield: about 9 dozen

Crème de Menthe Brownies

1 cup sugar
1 cup flour
1 (16-ounce) can chocolate
   syrup
$^1/_2$ cup butter, softened
4 eggs
1 teaspoon vanilla extract
$^1/_2$ teaspoon salt
5 tablespoons milk
3 tablespoons vanilla instant
   pudding mix
6 tablespoons melted butter
3 cups confectioners' sugar
2 tablespoons crème de menthe
1 cup semisweet
   chocolate chips
6 tablespoons butter

Combine the sugar, flour, chocolate syrup, $^1/_2$ cup butter, eggs, vanilla and salt in a bowl, mixing well. Pour into a greased 9x13-inch baking pan.

Bake at 350 degrees for 30 minutes. Cool completely on a wire rack.

Combine the milk and pudding mix in a bowl and beat until well blended. Add the melted butter and mix well. Add the confectioners' sugar and beat until fluffy. Stir in the crème de menthe. Spread over the cooled brownies. Refrigerate, covered.

Melt the chocolate chips and 6 tablespoons butter in a double boiler over hot water. Spread over the mint layer carefully. Refrigerate, covered, until the chocolate is firm. Cut into squares.

Yield: 12 to 15 servings

Galettes

1 1/2 cups melted butter
1 tablespoon shortening
1 1/2 cups packed brown sugar
1 1/2 cups sugar
1 tablespoon vanilla extract
1/8 teaspoon salt
6 eggs
4 cups flour

Beat the butter and shortening in a mixer bowl until creamy. Add the brown sugar and sugar gradually, beating well. Beat in the vanilla and salt. Add the eggs 1 at a time, beating well after each addition. Add the flour gradually, beating at low speed until blended.

Drop 1 tablespoon batter for each cookie onto an oiled and preheated electric waffle iron. (If using a standard waffle iron that makes 4 waffles, drop 1 tablespoon batter into each section.) Bake according to manufacturer's directions until golden brown. Remove to wire racks to cool. Store in an airtight container.

Note: Cookies will be about 2 inches in diameter. May increase the amount of batter per cookie to make larger cookies.

Yield: 5 dozen

Lemon Bars

1 cup flour
1/2 cup butter, softened
1/4 cup confectioners' sugar
2 eggs
1 cup sugar
3 tablespoons lemon juice
2 tablespoons flour
1/2 teaspoon baking powder
1/8 teaspoon salt

Cream the 1 cup flour, butter and confectioners' sugar in a bowl until well mixed. Press into a 9x9-inch baking pan.

Bake at 350 degrees for 15 minutes.

Combine the eggs, sugar, lemon juice, 2 tablespoons flour, baking powder and salt in a bowl and mix well. Pour over the baked crust.

Bake for 20 to 25 minutes or until set. Sprinkle with additional confectioners' sugar. Cool completely on a wire rack before cutting into bars.

Yield: 20 bars

A Special Knead

When it comes to dealing with difficult, and sometimes unpopular, social problems like alcoholism and drug abuse, the Junior League of Parkersburg has a history of filling a special need.

In the 1970s, local League members advocated for the treatment of alcohol and drug offenders and worked with other community organizations to establish a detoxification center. In the early 1990s, the organization mounted a campaign to educate the public about substance abuse among women by sponsoring lectures and producing and distributing informational literature.

But the Junior League's biggest undertaking in the area of substance abuse advocacy came with the development of the Women's Half Way House project. Half-way houses for men recovering from drug and/or alcohol dependency are common, but there were no facilities of this type for women in the entire state. The Junior League of Parkersburg worked to raise the funds necessary to build a facility where women could go to continue their recovery after they had been discharged from treatment.

The Junior League went on to win several area and national awards for their efforts in completing this project.

Salted Nut Bars

3 cups flour
1 1/2 cups packed brown sugar
1 cup margarine, softened
1 teaspoon salt
2 cups salted mixed nuts
1 cup butterscotch chips
1/2 cup light corn syrup
2 tablespoons margarine
1 tablespoon water

Combine the flour, brown sugar, 1 cup margarine and salt in a bowl, blending well. Press into a 10x15-inch baking pan.

Bake at 350 degrees for 10 to 12 minutes. Remove from the oven. Sprinkle the nuts over the surface.

Combine the butterscotch chips, corn syrup, 2 tablespoons margarine and water in a small saucepan. Bring to a boil. Boil for 2 minutes or until the chips are melted, stirring constantly. Pour evenly over the nuts.

Bake for 10 to 12 minutes or until golden brown. Cool completely on a wire rack. Cut into bars.

Yield: 4 dozen bars

Soft Sugar Cookies

2/3 cup shortening
1 1/4 cups sugar
2 eggs
1 tablespoon milk
1 teaspoon vanilla extract
3 cups flour
2 teaspoons baking powder
1 teaspoon salt

Cream the shortening and sugar in a bowl. Beat in the eggs, milk and vanilla. Add the flour, baking powder and salt and mix well. Refrigerate, covered, for 1 to 8 hours.

Roll out the dough on a lightly floured surface to a 1/4- to 1/8-inch thickness. Cut out with cookie cutters. Place 2 inches apart on cookie sheets.

Bake at 375 degrees for 8 to 10 minutes. Cool completely on wire racks. Decorate as desired.

Yield: about 4 dozen

Sand Tarts

1/2 cup butter, softened
1 cup sugar
2 eggs
1 3/4 cups flour
2 teaspoons baking powder
Cinnamon-sugar

Cream the butter and sugar in a bowl until light and fluffy. Beat in 1 of the eggs. Add the flour and baking powder and mix well. Shape the dough into a log. Wrap in plastic wrap. Refrigerate for 3 hours or until firm.

Slice the dough into rounds. Place 2 inches apart on cookie sheets. Beat the remaining egg. Brush over the surface of the cookies. Sprinkle with cinnamon-sugar.

Bake at 350 degrees for 10 minutes.

Yield: 2 dozen

Cranberry Streusel Pie

2 cups fresh or frozen
   cranberries
$1/4$ cup sugar
$1/4$ cup packed brown sugar
1 cup pecans, chopped
$1/2$ teaspoon cinnamon
1 unbaked (9-inch) pie shell
1 egg
$1/4$ cup melted butter or
   margarine
$1/3$ cup sugar
3 tablespoons flour

Combine the cranberries, $1/4$ cup sugar, brown sugar, pecans and cinnamon in a bowl. Spoon into the pie shell.

Whisk the egg, butter, $1/3$ cup sugar and flour in a bowl. Pour over the cranberry mixture.

Bake at 400 degrees for 20 minutes. Reduce the oven temperature to 350 degrees. Bake for 30 minutes.

Yield: 8 servings

Try

Fudge Nut Pie

2 (1-ounce) squares
   unsweetened chocolate
$1/4$ cup butter
$3/4$ cup sugar
$1/2$ cup packed light brown
   sugar
$1/2$ cup milk
3 eggs
$1/4$ cup corn syrup
1 teaspoon vanilla extract
$1/4$ teaspoon salt
1 cup finely chopped walnuts
1 unbaked (9-inch) pie shell

Heat the chocolate and butter in a 2-quart saucepan over low heat just until melted, stirring frequently. Remove from the heat. Whisk in the sugar, brown sugar, milk, eggs, corn syrup, vanilla and salt, blending well. Stir in the walnuts. Pour into the pie shell.

Bake at 350 degrees for 45 to 55 minutes or until the filling is puffed. Cool completely on a wire rack. Top each serving with a small scoop of coffee, vanilla or chocolate ice cream.

Yield: 6 servings

Grasshopper Pie

$2/3$ cup milk, scalded
24 large marshmallows
$1/4$ cup crème de menthe
2 tablespoons crème de cacao
1 cup whipping cream
1 chocolate cookie crumb crust

Combine the scalded milk and marshmallows in the top of a double boiler. Place over simmering water. Heat until the marshmallows are melted, stirring occasionally. Remove from the heat. Cool to room temperature. Stir in the crème de menthe and crème de cacao.

Beat the whipping cream until stiff peaks form. Fold into the marshmallow mixture. Spoon into the cookie crumb crust. Freeze, covered, until firm. Garnish with additional whipped cream and shaved chocolate.

Yield: 8 servings

Japanese Fruit Pie

1 cup sugar
2 eggs, lightly beaten
1/4 cup melted butter
1/2 cup flaked coconut
1/2 cup raisins
1/2 cup chopped pecans
1 tablespoon vinegar
1 unbaked (9-inch) pie shell

Combine the sugar, eggs, butter, coconut, raisins, pecans and vinegar in a bowl, mixing well. Spoon into the pie shell.

Bake at 350 degrees for 45 minutes or until a knife inserted in the center comes out clean. Serve with whipped topping, whipped cream or vanilla ice cream.

Yield: 6 to 8 servings

Key Lime Pie

4 egg whites
1 (14-ounce) can sweetened
  condensed milk
1/2 cup Key lime juice
1 graham cracker crumb crust

Beat the egg whites in a mixer bowl until stiff peaks form.

Combine the condensed milk and lime juice in a bowl. Fold in the beaten egg whites. Pour into the graham cracker crumb crust.

Freeze, covered, for 4 to 6 hours. Serve frozen with whipped topping if desired.

Yield: 6 servings

Mixed Berry Pie

6 cups fresh strawberries, sliced
2 cups fresh blueberries
2 cups fresh raspberries or
    blackberries
$1^{1}/_{2}$ cups sugar
5 tablespoons quick-cooking
    tapioca
$^{1}/_{4}$ teaspoon cinnamon
1 (10-inch) deep-dish pie shell
2 cups flour
$1^{1}/_{2}$ cups packed brown sugar
$^{1}/_{2}$ cup melted butter
2 teaspoons cinnamon
$^{1}/_{2}$ teaspoon salt

Combine the strawberries, blueberries, raspberries, sugar, tapioca and $^{1}/_{4}$ teaspoon cinnamon in a bowl. Spoon into the pie shell.

Combine the flour, brown sugar, butter, 2 teaspoons cinnamon and salt in a bowl, mixing until crumbly. Sprinkle over the top of the pie.

Bake at 350 degrees for 1 hour.

Yield: 8 servings

Peaches and Cream Pie

3 egg whites
1 cup sugar
12 (1x3-inch) butter crackers, crushed
1/2 cup chopped pecans
1 teaspoon vanilla extract
1/4 teaspoon baking powder
1 (29-ounce) can sliced peaches, drained
1 cup whipped cream

Beat the egg whites in a mixer bowl until foamy. Add the sugar gradually, beating until stiff peaks form. Fold in the butter cracker crumbs, pecans, vanilla and baking powder. Spread over the bottom and up the side of a buttered 10-inch pie plate.

Bake at 325 degrees for 30 minutes. Cool completely.

Fill the meringue crust with the peaches. Top with the whipped cream. Refrigerate, covered, for 2 to 8 hours before serving.

Yield: 8 servings

Florida Peanut Butter Pies

1 (18-ounce) jar creamy peanut butter
16 ounces cream cheese, softened
1 1/3 cups milk
1 (1-pound) package confectioners' sugar
16 ounces whipped topping
4 graham cracker crumb crusts

Combine the peanut butter, cream cheese, milk and confectioners' sugar in a very large bowl, mixing until smooth. Fold in the whipped topping. Spoon into the graham cracker crumb crusts, dividing evenly.

Freeze for at least 6 hours before serving. Garnish with chocolate candies and peanuts or chocolate curls, or drizzle with chocolate syrup.

Yield: 32 servings

Projects-To-Go

Our commitment towards enriching the lives of children has included various projects over the years. They include:

1951 . . . . established a Girl Scout Troop for homebound girls

1951–present . . . sponsored a girl to attend West Virginia Girls State

1971–73 . . . . . . served on the Community Advisory Board during the construction of the Juvenile Detention Home, and hosted the first open house

1983–87 . . . . . . designed activities for the residents of the Wood County Child Care Center and renovated living areas

1988–89 . . . . . . raised community awareness regarding teen sex and educated teens about their sexuality through the program "Peer Pressure Reversal"

1986–present . . opened the historic Cook House, headquarters of the Junior League of Parkersburg, for fourth-grade schoolchildren to tour

Try

Southern Pecan Pie

1/4 cup butter, softened
1 cup packed light brown sugar
1 cup light corn syrup
3 eggs
1/8 teaspoon salt
1 tablespoon flour
1 teaspoon vanilla extract
1/2 teaspoon cinnamon
1 unbaked (9-inch) pie shell
1 cup pecan halves

Cream the butter and brown sugar in a mixer bowl. Add the corn syrup and beat until light and fluffy. Whisk the eggs and salt in a bowl until light and fluffy. Add to the brown sugar mixture with the flour, vanilla and cinnamon and mix well. Pour into the pie shell. Sprinkle the pecans over the top.

Bake at 400 degrees for 10 minutes. Reduce the oven temperature to 350 degrees. Bake for 40 minutes.

Yield: 8 servings

_12/19/09_

Pecan Tassies

used butter

A Keeper

_160_

8 ounces cream cheese, softened
1 cup margarine, softened
2 cups flour
1 1/2 cups packed brown sugar
1 1/2 cups chopped pecans
2 eggs
3 tablespoons melted margarine
1 teaspoon vanilla extract
1/8 teaspoon salt

Combine the cream cheese, 1 cup margarine and flour in a bowl, mixing well. Shape the dough into 1-inch balls. Press 1 ball into each cup of miniature muffin pans to form a tart shell.

Combine the brown sugar, pecans, eggs, 3 tablespoons margarine, vanilla and salt in a bowl. Spoon 1 teaspoon into each tart shell.

Bake at 375 degrees for 15 minutes. Reduce the oven temperature to 300 degrees. Bake for 5 minutes.

Yield: 4 dozen

no vanilla used some almond. Prob. less

Good recipe. Make more than the Southern living one.

Divide dough in parts to determine size.

Pumpkin Pecan Pie

2 cups canned or mashed
   cooked pumpkin
4 eggs, lightly beaten
1 cup sugar
$1/2$ cup dark corn syrup
1 teaspoon vanilla extract
$1/2$ teaspoon salt
$1/2$ teaspoon cinnamon
1 unbaked (9-inch) pie shell
1 cup chopped pecans

Combine the pumpkin, eggs, sugar, corn syrup, vanilla, salt and cinnamon in a bowl, mixing well. Pour into the pie shell. Top with the pecans.

Bake at 350 degrees for 40 minutes or until set.

Yield: 8 servings

Swirled Pumpkin Tart

1 cup graham cracker crumbs
$1/4$ cup ground almonds
$1/4$ cup sugar
$1/4$ cup melted margarine
8 ounces cream cheese,
   softened
$3/4$ cup sugar
2 eggs
1 cup solid-pack canned
   pumpkin
$1^1/2$ teaspoons pumpkin pie
   spice

Combine the graham cracker crumbs, almonds, $1/4$ cup sugar and margarine in a bowl, stirring until all ingredients are moistened. Press over the bottom and up the side of a 9-inch pie plate. Refrigerate until chilled.

Beat the cream cheese and $3/4$ cup sugar in a bowl until smooth. Add the eggs and beat well. Reserve $1/2$ cup of the cream cheese batter in another bowl. Stir the pumpkin and pumpkin pie spice into the remaining batter. Pour into the prepared crust. Spoon the reserved batter over the pumpkin mixture. Swirl with a spoon.

Bake at 350 degrees for 40 to 50 minutes or until a knife inserted halfway between the outside edge and center comes out clean. Cool completely on a wire rack. Refrigerate, covered, until firm.

Yield: 10 servings

Special Strawberry Trifle

5 cups sliced fresh strawberries

2 (11-ounce) angel food cakes,
  cut into cubes

6 tablespoons plus 2 teaspoons
  strawberry schnapps

Rich Custard (page 163)

1/2 cup strawberry preserves

2 cups whipping cream

1/4 cup confectioners' sugar

1 tablespoon slivered almonds,
  toasted

Line the lower inside edge of a trifle bowl with some of the strawberry slices arranged cut side down. Arrange half the cake cubes in the bottom of the bowl. Sprinkle 2 tablespoons of the schnapps over the cake.

Combine the remaining strawberry slices with 2 tablespoons of the schnapps in a bowl. Let stand at room temperature for 30 minutes. Drain the strawberries, reserving 2 tablespoons of the liquid.

Top the cake in the trifle bowl with half of the drained strawberries. Spoon 2 cups of the chilled Rich Custard over the strawberry layer. Top with the remaining cake cubes and 2 tablespoons of the schnapps. Spoon the remaining strawberries over the cake.

Combine the preserves and reserved strawberry liquid in a bowl, stirring well. Spread over the top of the trifle. Spoon the remaining Rich Custard over the preserves.

Beat the whipping cream in a bowl until foamy. Add the confectioners' sugar gradually, beating until soft peaks form. Beat in the remaining 2 teaspoons schnapps. Spread the whipped cream over the top of the trifle. Top with the almonds and garnish with strawberry fans.

Rich Custard

1³/4 cups milk
1/4 cup plus 2 teaspoons
   cornstarch
2 cups half-and-half
4 egg yolks
3/4 cup sugar
2 teaspoons vanilla extract

Combine 1/2 cup of the milk and cornstarch in a large saucepan, blending well. Stir in the remaining 1¹/4 cups milk and half-and-half. Cook over medium heat until thickened, stirring constantly. Remove from the heat; set aside.

Beat the egg yolks and sugar in a mixer bowl at medium speed until thickened. Add 1/4 of the hot milk mixture gradually, beating constantly. Add the egg mixture gradually to the remaining milk mixture, stirring constantly. Cook over low heat for 1 to 2 minutes or until thickened, stirring constantly. Remove from the heat. Stir in the vanilla. Let cool at room temperature. Refrigerate, covered, until thoroughly chilled.

Yield: 14 servings

Cream Cheese Cherry Tarts

16 ounces cream cheese,
   softened
1¹/2 cups butter, softened
3 cups sifted flour
1 (14-ounce) can sweetened
   condensed milk
1/2 cup lemon juice
1 teaspoon vanilla extract
1 (21-ounce) can cherry pie
   filling

Beat 8 ounces of the cream cheese and the butter in a mixer bowl until light and fluffy. Stir in the flour to form a dough. Press the dough into miniature muffin cups, making indentations in the centers with your thumb to form tart shells. Bake at 350 degrees for 20 minutes. Cool completely and remove shells from muffin tin.

Beat the remaining 8 ounces cream cheese and condensed milk in a bowl. Add the lemon juice and vanilla, beating until smooth. Spoon the cream cheese filling into the cooled tart shells. Top each tart with a small amount of the pie filling, making sure that each tart has 1 or 2 cherries in the topping. Refrigerate, covered, until serving time.

Yield: about 4 dozen

French Apple Walnut Tart

Pâte Sucrée (page 165)
2 tablespoons strained apricot
    preserves, warmed
4 or 5 Granny Smith or
    Golden Delicious apples
    ($1^1/2$ to 2 pounds)
2 teaspoons fresh lemon juice
$1/2$ cup coarsely chopped
    walnuts
$2/3$ cup sugar
$1/4$ cup flour
$1/2$ teaspoon cinnamon
3 to 4 tablespoons unsalted
    butter, softened

Brush the Pâte Sucrée with the preserves while still warm.

Peel, halve and core the apples. Cut each apple half into $1/4$-inch-thick slices, keeping the slices intact in a half-apple shape. Sprinkle the apples with the lemon juice. Remove and coarsely chop the 2 end slices from each apple half. Spread the chopped apple over the bottom of the tart shell.

Arrange the remaining apple slices in the tart shell by starting at the outside edge and pointing them toward the center. Work around the outside edge, fanning out the slices evenly. Arrange a second row of apples inside the first, fanning them out in the opposite direction. Fill in the center with a few smaller apple slices. Sprinkle the walnuts over the apples.

Combine the sugar, flour and cinnamon in a small bowl. Add the butter, working it in with your fingertips to form a crumbly mixture. Sprinkle over the apples.

Place the tart on a large baking sheet. Bake at 400 degrees for 40 to 45 minutes or until golden brown.

Pâte Sucrée (Sweet Pastry Tart Shell)

1 1/2 cups flour
3 tablespoons superfine sugar
1/4 teaspoon salt
2/3 cup cold unsalted butter, cut
   into 1/2-inch cubes
1 egg, lightly beaten
1/2 teaspoon vanilla extract

Place the flour, sugar and salt in a food processor container. Pulse 3 or 4 times to blend. Distribute the butter around the bowl. Pulse 6 or 7 times. Process for 6 to 8 seconds or until the mixture resembles coarse meal.

Empty the crumbs onto a cool work surface. Form into a mound, making a 4-inch well in the center. Combine the egg and vanilla in a bowl. Pour into the well. Stir the crumbs into the egg mixture with a fork to form a dough. Cut the dough with a pastry blender to form large clumps. Shape into a loose ball.

Knead 2 to 3 tablespoons of the dough at a time, pushing outward in 6-inch sweeps. Repeat until all the dough is kneaded. Gather the dough into a loose ball again and repeat the kneading procedure twice.

Knead the dough with floured hands for 5 turns or until smooth. Shape into a 5-inch disk, dusting lightly with flour. Score the disk with the side of your hand. Wrap the dough in plastic wrap. Refrigerate for 20 minutes.

Roll out the dough on a lightly floured surface into a 14-inch circle. Fit into an 11-inch round tart pan with a removable bottom. Line the tart shell with foil and fill with dried beans or uncooked rice.

Bake at 425 degrees for 15 minutes. Remove the foil and beans. Bake for 5 to 10 minutes or until golden brown.

Yield: 10 to 12 servings

Apple Cinnamon Crisp

6 medium apples, peeled, sliced
1 cup packed light brown sugar
1 tablespoon lemon juice
1 to 2 tablespoons Grand
  Marnier (optional)
1 teaspoon dried lemon or
  orange peel
1 teaspoon ground cinnamon
1/2 cup flour
1/4 cup unsalted butter,
  softened
1/4 teaspoon nutmeg
1/2 cup chopped walnuts

Combine the apples, 1/2 cup of the brown sugar, lemon juice, Grand Marnier, lemon peel and 1/2 teaspoon of the cinnamon in a bowl. Spoon into a 1 1/2-quart shallow baking dish; set aside.

Combine the flour, remaining 1/2 cup brown sugar, butter, remaining 1/2 teaspoon cinnamon and nutmeg in a medium bowl, stirring until the mixture resembles coarse crumbs. Stir in the walnuts. Spread evenly over the apple mixture.

Bake at 375 degrees for 30 minutes. Serve with whipped cream or ice cream if desired.

Yield: 8 servings

Blueberry Crumble

1/3 cup packed brown sugar
2 tablespoons flour
1/2 teaspoon cinnamon
2 1/2 pints blueberries
2 tablespoons lemon juice
1/2 cup packed brown sugar
1/2 cup flour
1/4 cup butter or margarine
3/4 cup rolled oats

Combine the 1/3 cup brown sugar, 2 tablespoons flour and cinnamon in a bowl. Stir in the blueberries and lemon juice gently. Spoon into a greased 2-quart baking dish.

Combine the 1/2 cup brown sugar and 1/2 cup flour in a bowl. Cut in the butter until the mixture resembles coarse crumbs. Stir in the oats. Sprinkle evenly over the blueberry mixture.

Bake at 375 degrees for 40 minutes or until the topping is browned and the filling is bubbly. Serve with whipped cream or vanilla ice cream if desired.

Note: May substitute any of the following fruits for the blueberries: 2 1/2 pints raspberries or blackberries, 3 cups apples or peaches, or 4 cups cherries.

Yield: 8 servings

Try

Summer Harvest Cobbler

1/2 cup margarine
1 cup flour
1 cup sugar
1 cup milk
2 teaspoons baking powder
1 (21-ounce) can fruit or pie
    filling (any flavor)

Place the margarine in a 2-quart shallow baking dish. Place in a cold oven. Set the oven temperature to 325 degrees. Remove from the oven when the margarine is melted.

Combine the flour, sugar, milk and baking powder in a bowl, mixing until smooth. Pour into the center of the melted margarine. Do not stir. Pour the fruit or pie filling into the center of the batter. Do not stir.

Bake for 1 hour or until the top is browned. Serve with whipped cream if desired.

Yield: 8 servings

Halloween Haystacks

2 cups butterscotch chips
1 cup creamy or crunchy
  peanut butter
1 (5-ounce) can chow mein
  noodles
1 (10-ounce) can cashews or
  peanuts

Heat the butterscotch chips with the peanut butter in a saucepan over low heat until melted, stirring until smooth. Stir in the chow mein noodles and cashews.

Drop by tablespoonfuls onto waxed paper to form small haystacks. Let stand at room temperature until set.

Yield: about 3 dozen

Pot-of-Dirt Gardening Cake

1 (16-ounce) package cream-
  filled chocolate sandwich
  cookies
8 ounces fat-free or low-fat
  cream cheese, softened
1/4 cup corn oil margarine,
  softened
1 cup confectioners' sugar
2 large packages vanilla or
  banana instant pudding mix
3 1/2 cups skim milk
12 ounces whipped topping

Process the cookies in a blender or food processor container until ground and resembling potting soil; set aside.

Beat the cream cheese, margarine and confectioners' sugar in a bowl until smooth.

Prepare the pudding mix with the skim milk using package directions. Add to the cream cheese mixture and mix well. Fold in the whipped topping.

Layer the cookie crumbs and cream cheese mixture alternately in a clean, foiled-lined flowerpot, ending with the cookie crumbs. Insert a lightweight artificial flower. Serve with a clean garden trowel as a spoon.

Note: The cookies are easier to pulverize if they are first frozen.

Yield: 12 servings

Try

Pots de Crème

3/4 cup milk
1 cup semisweet
    chocolate chips
1 egg
2 tablespoons sugar
1 teaspoon vanilla extract
1/8 teaspoon salt
2 cups whipped cream

Heat the milk in a saucepan just to the boiling point. Pour into a blender container.

Add the chocolate chips, egg, sugar, vanilla and salt. Blend at low speed for 1 minute. Pour into individual pot de crème cups or custard cups. Refrigerate, covered, for 2 to 3 hours or until set. Serve with the whipped cream.

Yield: 6 servings

Chocolate Raspberry Bags

1 (10-ounce) package frozen
    raspberries, thawed, drained
1 cup confectioners' sugar
1 (17-ounce) package frozen
    puff pastry, thawed
1 cup semisweet
    chocolate chips
1 cup white chocolate chips
1 cup pecans, chopped
1/4 cup confectioners' sugar

Place the raspberries and 1 cup confectioners' sugar in a blender container. Process until smooth, stopping once to scrape down the sides of the container. Strain the raspberry mixture through a large sieve into a bowl. Discard the seeds. Refrigerate, covered, until chilled.

Roll each puff pastry sheet on a lightly floured surface to a 12-inch square. Cut each square into quarters.

Combine the semisweet chocolate chips, white chocolate chips and pecans in a bowl. Spoon an equal amount into the center of each pastry square, reserving a small amount for garnish if desired. Bring up the sides of the pastry squares to enclose the filling, twisting and pinching the pastry just above the filling to seal and form bags. Place on a baking sheet.

Bake at 425 degrees for 20 minutes. Swirl the raspberry sauce in a decorative manner on each serving plate. Place a chocolate raspberry bag in the center of each plate. Sift the 1/4 cup confectioners' sugar over the tops. Garnish with the reserved chocolate chip mixture.

Yield: 8 servings

White Chocolate Soufflé

2 tablespoons butter
1 1/2 tablespoons flour
2 ounces white chocolate
5 tablespoons sugar
1/2 cup milk, scalded
1/2 teaspoon vanilla extract
5 egg yolks
6 egg whites
Grand Marnier Sauce
   (page 171)

Melt the butter in a saucepan. Add the flour and stir until it just begins to turn golden; remove from the heat.

Add the white chocolate and 1 tablespoon of the sugar to the hot milk. Stir until the white chocolate is completely melted. Add to the flour mixture gradually, stirring constantly. Cook until thickened, stirring constantly. Cook for 5 minutes more, stirring constantly. Stir in the vanilla. Remove from the heat; set aside.

Beat the egg yolks with 3 tablespoons of the sugar in a bowl. Stir a small amount of the hot milk mixture into the egg yolks. Stir the egg yolk mixture gradually into the remaining milk mixture.

Beat the egg whites in a bowl until soft peaks form. Add the remaining 1 tablespoon sugar gradually, beating until stiff peaks form. Fold 1/4 of the beaten egg whites into the milk mixture. Add the remaining egg whites and fold in gently. Pour into a buttered and sugared soufflé dish.

Bake at 400 degrees for 20 minutes or at 350 degrees for 35 to 45 minutes. Serve immediately with Grand Marnier Sauce.

Yield: 6 servings

Grand Marnier Sauce

1 cup whole milk
1 vanilla bean, split lengthwise
  into halves
4 egg yolks
$1/2$ cup sugar
$3/4$ cup whipping cream
$1/8$ teaspoon salt
$1/4$ cup Grand Marnier

Combine the milk and vanilla bean in a saucepan. Heat until the milk is scalded. Remove the vanilla bean.

Beat the egg yolks in a bowl. Add to the hot milk gradually, beating constantly. Stir in the sugar. Blend in the whipping cream and salt. Pour into the top of a double boiler.

Heat over simmering water until the sauce mixture coats a metal spoon. Remove from the heat; cool slightly. Stir in the Grand Marnier.

Yield: about 2 $1/2$ cups

Raspberry Delight Cheesecake

2 cups graham cracker crumbs
1 cup toasted chopped almonds
$2/3$ cup melted butter
$1/2$ cup sugar
8 ounces cream cheese,
  softened
1 (14-ounce) can sweetened
  condensed milk
$1/3$ cup lemon juice
1 teaspoon vanilla extract
1 (6-ounce) package raspberry
  gelatin
2 cups boiling water
2 (10-ounce) packages frozen
  raspberries, partially thawed
2 cups whipped cream
$1/4$ cup toasted slivered
  almonds

Combine the graham cracker crumbs, 1 cup almonds, butter and sugar in a bowl. Press over the bottom of a 9x13-inch baking pan. Bake at 300 degrees for 10 minutes. Cool.

Beat the cream cheese, condensed milk, lemon juice and vanilla in a bowl until smooth. Pour over the prepared crust. Refrigerate, covered, until chilled.

Combine the gelatin and the boiling water in a bowl, stirring until the gelatin is completely dissolved. Add the raspberries and stir until completely thawed. Refrigerate until very thick. Pour over the cream cheese layer. Refrigerate, covered, until set.

Spread with the whipped cream and sprinkle with the $1/4$ cup almonds just before serving. Store, covered, in the refrigerator.

Yield: 16 to 20 servings

Sour Cherry and Peach Ginger Crisps

1¹/₂ pounds fresh cherries, pitted, or well-drained canned sour cherries

1 pound Greenbrier peaches, diced and well drained, or fresh ripe peaches, peeled and diced

¹/₂ cup sugar

1¹/₂ cups flour

1¹/₄ cups packed brown sugar

³/₄ cup unsalted butter, softened

1 cup rolled oats

2 tablespoons finely chopped crystallized ginger

Combine the cherries and peaches in a strainer or colander and drain again for 15 to 20 minutes. Toss the drained fruit with the sugar and 5 tablespoons of the flour in a bowl. Spoon into 8 buttered 1-cup ramekins or a buttered 2-quart baking dish; set aside.

Cream the brown sugar and butter in a bowl just until combined. Add the remaining 1 cup plus 3 tablespoons flour, oats and ginger. Stir just until blended; the mixture should be slightly lumpy. Crumble in an even layer over the fruit.

Bake at 375 degrees for 12 to 15 minutes for the ramekins or 15 to 18 minutes for the baking dish or until bubbly and the topping is browned. Cool slightly before serving.

Yield: 8 servings

Compliments of the Greenbrier Hotel

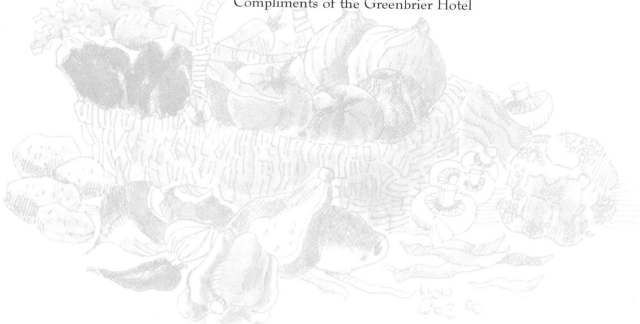

Pineapple Snowflake Delight

1 (2-layer) package yellow
  cake mix
1 (20-ounce) can juice-pack
  crushed pineapple
1 cup sugar
1 large package vanilla instant
  pudding mix
1 cup sour cream
8 ounces whipped topping

Prepare the cake mix and bake in a 9x13-inch baking pan using package directions. Punch holes over the surface of the cake with a fork.

Combine the undrained pineapple and sugar in a saucepan. Bring to a boil. Boil for 2 minutes. Spoon over the cake. Cool.

Prepare the pudding mix using package directions. Fold in the sour cream. Spread over the cooled cake. Top with the whipped topping. Garnish by sprinkling with shredded coconut, pecans and maraschino cherries.

Yield: 12 to 14 servings

Pumpkin Yummies

2 cups graham cracker crumbs
1/2 cup melted unsalted butter
1/4 cup sugar
2 cups solid-pack canned
  pumpkin
1/2 cup packed light
  brown sugar
1 teaspoon cinnamon
1/2 teaspoon salt
1/4 teaspoon ginger
1/4 teaspoon ground cloves
1 quart vanilla ice cream,
  softened
Brown sugar
Cinnamon
Sugar

Combine the graham cracker crumbs, butter and 1/4 cup sugar in a 9x13-inch baking pan. Spread evenly over the bottom of the pan.

Combine the pumpkin, 1/2 cup brown sugar, 1 teaspoon cinnamon, salt, ginger and cloves in a large bowl, mixing well. Fold in the ice cream. Spoon over the graham cracker crust, smoothing with a spatula. Combine additional brown sugar, cinnamon and sugar in a bowl. Sprinkle over the top. Cover with plastic wrap. Freeze until firm.

Yield: 15 servings

Warm Blueberry Sauce

1/3 cup packed brown sugar
1 tablespoon cornstarch
1/2 teaspoon cinnamon
1/8 teaspoon ground cloves
1/4 cup water
2 tablespoons lemon juice
2 cups fresh blueberries

Combine the brown sugar, cornstarch, cinnamon and cloves in a microwave-safe dish. Add the water and lemon juice gradually, whisking until blended. Stir in the blueberries.

Microwave on High for 5 to 6 minutes or until thickened and bubbly, stirring every 2 minutes. Serve over ice cream, pancakes or waffles.

Yield: 1 3/4 cups

Fudge Sauce

4 ounces unsweetened
   chocolate
1 (5-ounce) can evaporated
   milk
1/2 teaspoon salt
1/2 teaspoon vanilla extract
2 cups confectioners' sugar

Melt the chocolate in a medium saucepan over low heat. Add the evaporated milk, salt and vanilla, stirring constantly. Add the confectioners' sugar gradually, cooking until smooth and stirring constantly. Serve warm.

Note: May be refrigerated, covered, and reheated in the microwave oven.

Yield: about 2 cups

Beverages

Beverages

Champagne Punch

1 (6-ounce) can frozen
   lemonade concentrate
2 (6-ounce) cans frozen
   pineapple juice
6 (6-ounce) cans cold water
1 (750-milliliter) bottle
   riesling, chilled
1 (750-milliliter) bottle
   Champagne, chilled
4 cups frozen whole
   strawberries

Combine the lemonade concentrate, pineapple juice and water in a large punch bowl. Stir in the wine and Champagne. Float the strawberries on top just before serving.

Yield: 25 servings

Raspberry and Champagne Punch

1 (6-ounce) can frozen
   lemonade concentrate
1/2 cup water
1 (10-ounce) package frozen
   raspberries
1 (1-liter) bottle lemon-lime
   soda, chilled
1 (750-milliliter) bottle
   Champagne, chilled

Combine the lemonade concentrate and water in a punch bowl, stirring until the concentrate is completely dissolved. Add the raspberries, soda and Champagne; mix gently. Ladle into punch cups.

Yield: 24 servings

Raspberry Sherbet Punch

2 (12-ounce) cans frozen pink
   lemonade concentrate,
   thawed
1/2 gallon raspberry sherbet,
   softened
2 (2-liter) bottles ginger ale,
   chilled

Combine the lemonade concentrate and sherbet in a punch bowl. Stir in the ginger ale, breaking up the sherbet. Garnish with an ice ring filled with cherries and sliced lemons and limes. Serve immediately.

Yield: 50 servings

Sangria Blanco

1 gallon chablis
1/2 to 1 cup brandy
3 apples and/or pears
3 quarts ginger ale

Pour the wine and brandy into a large container. Slice the fruit; do not peel. Add to the brandy mixture. Chill in the refrigerator for 1 hour or longer. Pour into a punch bowl when ready to serve. Add the ginger ale and ice.

Yield: 38 servings

A-Whole-Lot-of-Fun Margaritas

1 (6-ounce) can frozen limeade
   concentrate
1 limeade can beer
1 limeade can tequila
Ice

Place the limeade concentrate in a blender container. Add the beer and tequila. Add desired amount of ice. Process until blended. Garnish glasses with salt and lime slices. To garnish glasses, dip rims into lime juice then into coarsely ground salt. Add lime slices.

Note: For less fun, use less tequila.

Yield: 4 servings

Lemonade Punch

2 (3-ounce) packages lemon gelatin
2 cups boiling water
2 (12-ounce) cans frozen orange juice concentrate
2 (6-ounce) cans frozen lemonade concentrate
2 (48-ounce) cans pineapple juice
1 tablespoon almond extract
2 (1-liter) bottles lemon-lime soda

Dissolve the gelatin in the boiling water in a large bowl. Stir in the orange juice concentrate, lemonade concentrate, pineapple juice, almond extract and soda. Pour into a punch bowl. Add an ice ring to chill.

Yield: 50 servings

Fresh-Squeezed Lemonade

1 1/2 cups hot water
1 1/2 cups freshly squeezed lemon juice
1 1/2 cups sugar
1 tablespoon grated lemon zest
Club soda or water

Combine the hot water, lemon juice, sugar and lemon zest in a 1-quart jar. Cover and shake until the sugar is completely dissolved. Refrigerate for 2 hours or longer.

Mix 1/4 cup lemon juice mixture with 3/4 cup club soda or water for each serving of lemonade.

Note: The lemon juice mixture may be stored in the refrigerator for up to 1 week.

Yield: 16 servings

Merry Berry Mint Cooler

4 scoops vanilla ice cream
1/4 cup half-and-half
1 tablespoon (heaping)
    cranberries
5 small mint patties
Whipped cream

Place the ice cream, half-and-half, cranberries and mint patties in a blender container. Process until blended and creamy. Pour into 2 wine glasses. Top with whipped cream. Garnish with small candy canes and mint sprigs.

Yield: 2 servings

Brandy Slush

2 cups water
2 cups sugar
2 green tea bags
2 cups boiling water
1 (12-ounce) can frozen
    lemonade concentrate
1 (12-ounce) can frozen orange
    juice concentrate
2 cups brandy
Lemon-lime soda or ginger ale

Combine the 2 cups water and sugar in a large saucepan. Bring to a boil. Boil until the sugar is completely dissolved.

Steep the tea bags in the 2 cups boiling water. Add the brewed tea to the sugar mixture. Stir in the lemonade concentrate, orange juice concentrate and brandy. Pour into a freezer container. Freeze until slushy.

Scoop slush into glasses when ready to serve. Add enough soda to fill the glasses.

Yield: 15 servings

Strawberry Slush

4 ounces strawberry de
    bordeaux
2 ounces rum
2 teaspoons lemon juice
1 cup frozen strawberries,
    partially thawed

Place the liqueur, rum, lemon juice and strawberries in a blender container. Blend for 15 seconds. Serve in chilled goblets.

Yield: 2 servings

Cocoa Chill Chaser Mix

1 (14-ounce) package nonfat
   dry milk powder
1 (16-ounce) jar powdered
   creamer
1 (32-ounce) package chocolate
   drink mix
1/3 cup confectioners' sugar

Combine the milk powder, creamer, drink mix and confectioners' sugar in a bowl; blend well. Store in an airtight container. Combine 1/3 cup chocolate mixture with 1 cup hot water for each serving of hot chocolate.

Yield: 40 to 45 servings

Christmas Eve Wassail

2 1/2 cups pineapple juice
2 cups cranberry juice cocktail
1/2 cup water
1/3 cup packed brown sugar
1/2 teaspoon whole cloves
1/2 teaspoon whole allspice
3 cinnamon sticks

Combine the pineapple juice, cranberry juice and water in a large saucepan. Mix in the brown sugar. Place the cloves and allspice in a tea ball. Add to the juice mixture with the cinnamon sticks. Heat over low heat until warm. Remove the tea ball and cinnamon sticks. Serve warm.

Yield: 8 servings

Hot Spiced Cider

4 cups apple cider
2/3 cup packed brown sugar
2 small cinnamon sticks
8 whole cloves
1/4 teaspoon nutmeg
1/4 teaspoon ginger

Combine the cider, brown sugar, cinnamon sticks, cloves, nutmeg and ginger in a saucepan. Bring to a boil, stirring constantly. Reduce the heat to low. Simmer for 10 minutes. Remove the cinnamon sticks and cloves. Serve warm.

Yield: 8 servings

Touchdown Tailgating Mix

4^1/$_2$ cups tomato juice
Lemon juice to taste
Garlic powder taste
Pepper to taste
Salt to taste
Soy sauce to taste
Texas Pete hot sauce or
   Tabasco sauce to taste
6 shots vodka
6 celery ribs

Combine the tomato juice, lemon juice, garlic powder, pepper, salt and hot sauce in a bowl. Taste and adjust the seasonings. Serve chilled or over ice. Add a celery rib to each glass.

Yield: 6 servings

Homemade Bailey's Irish Cream

1 (14-ounce) can sweetened
   condensed milk
2 cups half-and-half
1 cup whiskey or brandy
^{1}/$_3$ cup rum
3 eggs
2 tablespoons chocolate syrup
1 teaspoon vanilla extract

Combine the condensed milk, half-and-half, whiskey, rum, eggs, chocolate syrup and vanilla in a blender container. Blend until well mixed. Pour into a covered container. Refrigerate until ready to serve.

Note: May store in refrigerator up to the shelf-life date on the half-and-half. May substitute pasteurized egg substitute for the 3 eggs.

Yield: 10 to 12 servings

Contributors

The committee wishes to express their appreciation to the following friends who generously contributed recipes for our book. Unfortunately, due to space and cost limitations we were not able to publish all recipes received. We hope our active and sustaining members will understand the compromises that had to be made and will share in our excitement over the finished product.

Mrs. C. Wallace
    Anderson
Tricia Armiger
Sara Bailey
Mary Bango
Peg Barlament
Suzanne Evans Beane
Ellen Boone
Jane E. Burdette
Christine Calkins
Michelle Camp
Molly Cigal
Marian Clowes
Kim Couch
Laura Coyne
Judy Crichton
Teresa Crumbaker
Sharon Walker Davis
Jane Dils
Susan Dolinar
Lisa Dowless
Pamela Evans
Judith Fahlgren
Kathy Ferrell
Vicky Ferry
Barbara Fish

Anne Garvin
Cynthia Gissy
Kathleen Glasscock
Michelle Goodman
The Greenbrier Hotel
Mrs. Van L. Hall
Terry Hardman
Betsy Hawthorne
Julie Heller
Karen E. Herring
Brenda Hoffman
Sherry Hunter
Judy Langkamer
Dolores Lee
Kelly L. Lee
Mickey Lewis
D'Ann Duesterhoeft
    McGraw
Paula McHenry
Debbie McKitten
Ellen V. Mesaros
Cynthia Meyers
Carolyn Miller
Heidi Montemurro
Melissa Moore
Carol R. Olson

Lisa Parrill Onestinghel
Donna Jean Pamfilis
Arlene Parsons
Kathy H. Parsons
Jean Pearcy
Stacia A. Pierce
Sharon Plauche
Annette Queen
Lora Quillen
Carol Ramsey
Judith Young Rathbone
Carrie L. Reed
Dawn R. Root
Tina Salmans
Tricia Sanders
Carol Seufer
Anne Cawley Smith
Barbara D. Smith
Caroline Smith
Erin Snider
Toni Tiano
Tracy M. Wharton
Val Woofter
Becky Young

Equivalent Chart

When the recipe calls for	Use

Baking

$1/2$ cup butter	4 ounces
2 cups butter	1 pound
4 cups all-purpose flour	1 pound
$4^{1}/_{2}$ to 5 cups sifted cake flour	1 pound
1 square chocolate	1 ounce
1 cup semisweet chocolate chips	6 ounces
4 cups marshmallows	1 pound
$2^{1}/_{4}$ cups packed brown sugar	1 pound
4 cups confectioners' sugar	1 pound
2 cups sugar	1 pound

Cereal/Bread/Grain

1 cup fine dry bread crumbs	4 to 5 slices
1 cup soft bread crumbs	2 slices
1 cup small bread cubes	2 slices
1 cup fine cracker crumbs	28 saltines
1 cup fine graham cracker crumbs	15 crackers
1 cup vanilla wafer crumbs	22 wafers
1 cup crushed cornflakes	3 cups uncrushed
4 cups cooked macaroni	8 ounces uncooked
$3^{1}/_{2}$ cups cooked rice	1 cup uncooked

Dairy

1 cup shredded cheese	4 ounces
1 cup cottage cheese	8 ounces
1 cup sour cream	8 ounces
1 cup whipped cream	$1/2$ cup whipping cream
$2/3$ cup evaporated milk	1 small can
$1^{2}/_{3}$ cups evaporated milk	1 (13-ounce) can

Fruit

4 cups sliced or chopped apples	4 medium
1 cup mashed bananas	3 medium
$2^{1}/_{2}$ cups shredded coconut	8 ounces
4 cups cranberries	1 pound
1 cup pitted dates	1 (8-ounce) package
1 cup candied fruit	1 (8-ounce) package
3 to 4 tablespoons lemon juice plus 1 tablespoon grated lemon peel	1 lemon
$1/3$ cup orange juice plus 2 teaspoons grated orange peel	1 orange

4 cups sliced peaches..8 medium
2 cups pitted prunes ....1 (12-ounce) package
3 cups raisins...1 (15-ounce) package

Meats
4 cups chopped cooked chicken ....1 (5-pound) chicken
3 cups chopped cooked meat..1 pound, cooked
2 cups cooked ground meat..1 pound, cooked

Nuts
1 cup chopped nuts ....4 ounces shelled or
                                                                          1 pound unshelled

Vegetables
2 cups cooked green beans ....$^1/_2$ pound fresh or
                                                                          1 (16-ounce) can
$2^1/_2$ cups lima beans or red beans................................1 cup dried, cooked
4 cups shredded cabbage ....1 pound
1 cup grated carrot..1 large
8 ounces fresh mushrooms ....1 (4-ounce) can
1 cup chopped onion..1 large
4 cups sliced or chopped potatoes.....................................4 medium
2 cups canned tomatoes ....1 (16-ounce) can

Measurement Equivalents

1 tablespoon = 3 teaspoons
2 tablespoons = 1 ounce
4 tablespoons = $^1/_4$ cup
$5^1/_3$ tablespoons = $^1/_3$ cup
8 tablespoons = $^1/_2$ cup
12 tablespoons = $^3/_4$ cup
16 tablespoons = 1 cup
1 cup = 8 ounces or $^1/_2$ pint
4 cups = 1 quart
4 quarts = 1 gallon

1 ($6^1/_2$- to 8-ounce) can = 1 cup
1 ($10^1/_2$- to 12-ounce) can = $1^1/_4$ cups
1 (14- to 16-ounce) can = $1^3/_4$ cups
1 (16- to 17-ounce) can = 2 cups
1 (18- to 20-ounce) can = $2^1/_2$ cups
1 (29-ounce) can = $3^1/_2$ cups
1 (46- to 51-ounce) can = $5^3/_4$ cups
1 ($6^1/_2$- to $7^1/_2$-pound) can or
Number 10 = 12 to 13 cups

Metric Equivalents

Liquid
1 teaspoon = 5 milliliters
1 tablespoon = 15 milliliters
1 fluid ounce = 30 milliliters
1 cup = 250 milliliters
1 pint = 500 milliliters

Dry
1 quart = 1 liter
1 ounce = 30 grams
1 pound = 450 grams
2.2 pounds = 1 kilogram

Substitution Chart

Instead of	Use
Baking	
1 teaspoon baking powder	1/4 teaspoon baking soda plus 1/2 teaspoon cream of tartar
1 tablespoon cornstarch (for thickening)	2 tablespoons flour or 1 tablespoon tapioca
1 cup sifted all-purpose flour	1 cup plus 2 tablespoons sifted cake flour
1 cup sifted cake flour	1 cup minus 2 tablespoons sifted all-purpose flour
Bread Crumbs	
1 cup dry bread crumbs	3/4 cup cracker crumbs
Dairy	
1 cup buttermilk	1 cup sour milk or 1 cup yogurt
1 cup whipping cream	3/4 cup milk plus 1/3 cup butter
1 cup light cream	7/8 cup skim milk plus 3 tablespoons butter
1 cup sour cream	7/8 cup sour milk plus 3 tablespoons butter
1 cup sour milk	1 cup milk plus 1 tablespoon vinegar or lemon juice, or 1 cup buttermilk
Seasoning	
1 teaspoon allspice	1/2 teaspoon cinnamon plus 1/8 teaspoon cloves
1 cup catsup	1 cup tomato sauce plus 1/2 cup sugar plus 2 tablespoons vinegar
1 garlic clove	1/8 teaspoon garlic powder or 1/8 teaspoon instant minced garlic or 3/4 teaspoon garlic salt or 5 drops of liquid garlic
1 teaspoon Italian spice	1/4 teaspoon each oregano, basil, thyme, rosemary plus dash of cayenne
1 teaspoon lemon juice	1/2 teaspoon vinegar
1 tablespoon mustard	1 teaspoon dry mustard
1 medium onion	1 tablespoon dried minced onion or 1 teaspoon onion powder
Sweet	
1 (1-ounce) square chocolate	1/4 cup baking cocoa plus 1 teaspoon shortening
1 2/3 ounces semisweet chocolate	1 ounce unsweetened chocolate plus 4 teaspoons sugar
1 cup honey	1 to 1 1/4 cups sugar plus 1/4 cup liquid, or 1 cup corn syrup or molasses
1 cup sugar	1 cup packed brown sugar, or 1 cup corn syrup, molasses or honey minus 1/4 cup liquid

Index

Everything But The Entrée

The Junior League of Parkersburg, Inc.
P.O. Box 4051
Parkersburg, West Virginia 26104
304-422-6961

Please send me _____ copies of Everything But The Entrée at $19.95 each $ _____

Postage and handling at $3.00 each $ _____

West Virginia residents add 6% sales tax $ _____

Total $ _____

_____
Name

_____
Street Address

_____
City   State   Zip

( )
_____
Daytime Telephone

Method of Payment: [   ] VISA   [   ] MasterCard

                        [   ] Check enclosed payable to The Junior League of Parkersburg, Inc.

_____
Account Number   Expiration Date

_____
Cardholder Name

_____
Signature

Photocopies accepted.